Dying To Live

Embracing The Journey

Joanne Harvey MSW

authorHOUSE®

AuthorHouse™
1663 Liberty Drive
Bloomington, IN 47403
www.authorhouse.com
Phone: 1-800-839-8640

The information in this book is a result of years working as a hospice social worker. It is intended to educate through story telling. Each hospice agency is different and may or may not provide all the services referred to in this book. If you believe you need medical intervention, please see a medical practitioner as soon as possible. The stories in Dying to Live are true. Names and circumstances have been changed to protect the anonymity of patients and their families. If any story or incident described in this book seems familiar it is because these experiences occur in many families in similar situations.

First published by AuthorHouse 9/3/2010
ISBN: 978-1-4520-4749-2 (e)
ISBN: 978-1-4520-4750-8 (sc)
ISBN: 978-1-4520-4751-5 (hc)

Printed in the United States of America

All photographs © Jim Reynolds or Joanne Harvey

Cover photo © Joanne Harvey 2010

Cover design by Angela Treat Lyon

Acknowledgements

I am blessed to have so many loving friends and family to thank, for their encouragement and guidance.

First, I would like to thank the incredible hospice staff with whom I have had the privilege to work. Their sense of humor, compassion and dedication to excellent patient care is remarkable and I am honored to be part of the team.

I thank all the hospice patients who have allowed me to stand in the fire with them. If it wasn't for these brave souls and their families and their willingness to be open to the journey, this book would never have been written.

I thank my mother, Bettye, and my sister, Kathleen, for taking the time to read my work and not being afraid to tell the truth. Pam Kerr, my dear friend, who is always there for me, you are amazing. And Angela Treat Lyon, who provided me with the impetus to complete a dream.

And a very special thank you to Percy McManus, who has kept me healthy for years and truly understood this project from day one.

Immortality

Do not stand at my grave and weep
I am not there I do not sleep
I am a thousand winds that blow
I am a diamond glint in the snow
I am the sunlight on ripened grain
I am the gentle autumn's rain
When you awake in the morning hush
I am the swift uplifting rush of quiet birds in circle
flight. I am the soft stars that shine at night
Do no stand on my grave and cry
I am not there I did not die

UNKNOWN

This book is dedicated to
Jim
my wonderful husband
who has taught me
what living life to the fullest
is all about.

Forgiveness is all about giving up the possibility of a better past.
It's your life, start with today and make it a wonderful future.

James Caldwell Harvey

Contents

Introduction xi

The Scent of Honey 1

Leaving on Friday 11

Carrots, Eggs, and Coffee 21

When Someone Cares 25

The Kindness of Strangers..37

For The Love of Family 69

Tapping into the Present--A Love Story...87

Finding Honor 99

Jack and the DragonFly 115

Resources 125

Recommended Reading..130

What are Meridian Tapping Techniques? 135

Think of all the beauty that's still left in and around you and be happy!

ANNE FRANK

Introduction

End of life issues impact us all. No one gets out of here alive. In your lifetime and mine we will see loved ones die, and one day we will be the one dying.

Dying to Live is a collection of true stories about real people living with a terminal illness. These are empowering stories that help embrace life and release fear.

Dying to Live is about transitions. It's about preparing for death, honoring the process and living with eyes wide open. It's about dealing with fear while problem solving, celebrating accomplishments, tapping into the present with gratitude and consciously living life.

Dying to Live is about the hospice team helping to make it all happen. Death is discussed openly and honestly, and a new freedom is found. You get to make up your own rules and take control of what is left of your life, and make it count!

I invite you to use *Dying to Live* to find the answers you are looking for, and identify questions you didn't know you could ask.

I encourage you to ask your doctor about hospice services. Hospice care is available to anyone in the United States and some other parts of the world who has been diagnosed with a life-limiting illness.

Through these real-life inspiring stories you will gain the confidence you need to look at your own eventual death and still live life to the fullest.

Author's Note

We've been living and dying since humans have walked on this earth. No one really wants to think about it, but we all die. I wrote this book to speak directly about this last major event in all our lives. By recognizing our mortality, we can make our wishes clear, and plan the end of our life with the same amount of passion and care as we take living it.

I wrote **Dying to Live** because my life has been extraordinarily changed by looking into the eyes of people who are dying. I am no longer afraid to die. However, I am bothered that I probably won't complete all my projects before that inevitable moment. It is that realization that has pushed me to write this book. It is the courage and honesty of these dying patients, along with their families and friends which compels me to share these stories.

I am often asked how I handle my own emotions while guiding individuals at the end of their lives. I'd like to say that my professionalism keeps me apart from my patients and their families, but that would be a lie. I do carry their stories for a while, some longer than others, but I remind myself that their story is not my journey. I do not walk their path, I walk beside it. In doing so, I can hold their hand, stand in the fire, and consciously support living in the present. It is my job to encourage understanding and love as long as life is possible. I am honored to explore the meaning of life as a hospice social worker and to help the dying find opportunities to encourage family communication and heal the past.

I am always in awe of the glow that radiates from a person who is dying and accepts it. Although I am not a priest or a member of the clergy, spiritual experiences are discussed. I have consciously kept religious identifiers out of these stories, because hospice honors all beliefs, regardless of their affiliations.

I hope that everyone who reads these stories is touched by the similarity of beliefs. Each story reveals the remarkable courage of patients and their families as they face the challenges of living for each moment that is left, and how peace can be recovered.

If you or someone you know is challenged by a terminal illness, consider calling the nearest hospice facility. They will gladly answer any questions you have. You will find resources and contact information on page 125.

All we have is the present. None of us has a crystal ball to know when we will die. But the fact is we will. Let's all make plans, talk about our death and what we want at the end of our life. It's OK; we're in this together. It's nice to know hospice will help support our quality of life when that time comes.

Wishing you a full and happy life!

To be what we are, and to become what we are capable of becoming, is the only way of life.

ROBERT LOUIS STEVENSON

CHAPTER 1

The Scent of Honey

When the hospice intake team drove up to the log cabin, children were playing in the yard. A little girl wearing a big yellow hat stopped and looked curiously at the ladies who had invaded her play time. She took off her hat, and Dalia's beautiful   lavender eyes defined her face. A face that had seen it all in her four short years of life--but was determined to ignore the impact.

Dalia was the only girl in her family, second to the last of seven children. Her laughter sounded like a fairy bell. Her brothers, even the youngest, towered over her, but she was obviously the one in charge, directing play with her tiny hands and running through the wet grass in her black patent leather shoes.

Dalia ran with her mouth open and her hands outstretched, as if she was trying to grab every bit of life she could. She had been cancer-free for eighteen months, but now it had come back with a vengeance. This time it was throughout her body. She had tumors on her femur and in her lungs, and the doctors said there was nothing else they could do.

Dalia's parents, John and Debbie, fought the prognosis for more than eight months, doing everything they could to keep their sweet little girl alive. Debbie was a skilled, self-taught nurse, receiving her education from doing, rather than going to school for it. She knew everything medically that had to be done for her daughter. She could draw blood, start an IV, tube feed, bandage and even soothe and sing songs right in the middle of crisis. But the oncologist's prediction was the hardest thing Dalia's parents faced.

When hospice was suggested by the doctor, at first John and Debbie refused. "She is doing just fine, thank you." They didn't want to give up hope for their daughter.

Hope can be such a loaded word, one that means so many things. You can hope to see your children grow up to be happy. You can hope to always do your best. You can hope for many things, but when someone, no matter what age, is dealing with a life-threatening illness your hopes change significantly. You do not want to see your loved one suffer. Sometimes hope is simply that my little girl gets to live with love and laughter with the least amount of pain, for as long as possible.

Eventually Debbie realized that her daughter needed more help than she could provide. Often Dalia's pain could not be controlled and Debbie could see her little girl was losing the fight. After discussing it with John, she bravely called hospice.

We were invited into the house and explained to John and Debbie that hospice is a support team, a group of trained individuals who are committed to enhancing the excellent care that Debbie was already providing. John and Debbie eventually understood that hospice was not just a medical team, but people who would celebrate Dalia's successes, be her advocate, be the doctor's eyes and ears and support the family during the difficult days ahead.

Coincidentally and unexpectedly, on the same day hospice was introduced to Dalia, Debbie discovered she was pregnant.

One month later Dalia was told the news first. She was so happy; she was finally going to have a sister! She was even given the honor of naming the baby.

After much deliberation, Dalia decided to name her Purple Sage. Dalia proudly announced that she had named her new baby sister, still in her mommy's tummy, and that the baby would be called Sage, for short.

Each time she announced the news, she always giggled her tiny belllike giggle. Why she decided on this name no one really knew. Purple was her favorite color, but Sage was not a word Dalia normally used. She loved it, though, and she knew Purple Sage would love it too.

Dalia was very social. It became obvious in our first meeting that she knew what she liked, and wasn't afraid to tell me. She said she loved kitties, especially the white ones. She liked her brothers, but they were pretty silly most of the time, and she liked vanilla ice cream with blackberries on top.

Dalia would tell me that her favorite thing "in the whole wide world" was to ride with her family on their four-wheeler. When she was riding, she said she felt free and loved because everyone was together, arms around each other, everybody happy.

Her favorite place to ride on these family adventures was up the canyon not far from her home, where a natural spring bubbled out from a huge boulder, and wild purple butterfly plants grew with abandon.

She told me in a whisper, "Did you know fairies live in those butterfly bushes? The way you can tell that fairies are there is from the sweet honey smell."

She giggled when her brothers disputed the fairy stories. Her look plainly said, they're just boys, how would they know?

The summer was sweet for the family, cool breezes and lazy days of playing in the yard. Dalia's tumors grew, but most of the time Debbie controlled her child's discomfort with medication and buckets of love.

In the fall, Dalia's decline was rapid. Debbie found that she needed the hospice team to visit more often for support. The nurses were there daily to deal with Dalia's symptoms and the constantly increasing pain.

I visited regularly for emotional support and encouraged John and Debbie to talk about Dalia's journey. Even though she was first diagnosed before she was a year old, they still struggled with the devastating news.

Debbie and John lived a very healthy lifestyle. There was no reason why cancer had touched their little girl. But most of all we talked about Dalia's amazing bravery and her great personality, even with the monumental challenges she faced daily. We talked about the wonderful lessons her parents received from their child about living life to the fullest.

I spoke about the end, preparing them for the time they would have to say goodbye to their sweet Dalia.

Debbie tearfully said, "Dalia's always been a free spirit. I just want my little girl to go without pain."

We talked more about what they both saw physically happening to Dalia. John said, with his hands clenched into fists, "If I could trade places, I would in a second, but since I can't, I just want her to go gently. But," he said crying, "when I say those words I feel like I am letting my little girl go without a fight!"

Debbie wrapped her arms around her husband and held him as he sobbed with frustration.

Dalia's condition continued to deteriorate and required daily visits from the hospice nurse. The family tried to stay balanced, even with the awful circumstances playing out in their home.

Debbie and John made a point to play with all the kids in the living room at the end of the day. This day, despite very strong medication, Dalia was still in significant pain. But Dalia loved the family evening time and asked Debbie in a whisper if she could join everyone.

Debbie watched as John tenderly picked up his tiny little girl and gingerly carried her into the living room. Her brothers didn't seem to notice how heroic this simple act was, not only for their father but also for Dalia. She wanted to be with her family!

Even in her discomfort Dalia was able to boss her oldest brother, Josh, and get him to sit quietly so she could be in his lap.

Josh was 12 and big for his age. Dalia looked like a tiny doll in his lap. He was gentle with her, holding her as if she was a little glass figurine. He was very aware of what was happening, his brown eyes full of love and deep sadness. He had watched his baby sister fight this disease since he was eight. He teased her a little for bossing him around and then held still while she whispered a sassy reply that only he could hear. He smiled and looked up at his Dad, as if to say, can this really be happening?

The evening ended like all the others; each hugging and saying good night. But John and Debbie knew this would most likely be one of their last nights, all of them together.

Just after midnight, Debbie heard Dalia softly calling and quietly stepped into her room.

Dalia was wide awake, her hospital bed full of stuffed toys. Her baby brother, Robert, had even added some of his own toys before he went to bed.

Surprised to find her awake, Debbie listened carefully as Dalia asked to be taken for a ride. She wanted to ride on their four-wheeler. Debbie couldn't believe Dalia would be asking to be moved at all--her pain was always just under the surface, and to be moved would be excruciatingly painful. But that was exactly what she was requesting.

Dalia whispered again, "Mommy, take me for a ride, I want to see the fairies."

Debbie told me later that she stood there for a long time, trying to remember her little girl's face, but all she saw was an angel who had been through too much.

She got dressed, and then went back into her daughter's room and gathered her in warm blankets.

Dalia cried out a little and when Debbie tried to put her back into bed, Dalia begged, "No, Mommy, I want to see the fairies!"

Debbie walked out into the autumn night, holding Dalia, keeping her warm with a blanket around her little body.

Debbie carefully swung her leg over the seat of the four-wheeler and slowly started down the gravel road, the road that led to the bubbling spring and the purple butterfly bushes. Dalia didn't complain, she just leaned back into her mother's warmth and sighed deeply.

Debbie slowly, cautiously, drove into the night, remembering the terrifying and heartbreaking journey she and Dalia had been through.

They arrived at the spring and could hear the water cheerfully bubbling out of the crack in the earth. A cool breeze rustled the butterfly bushes, their leaves reflecting silver in the moonlight.

Dalia cried out when Debbie tried to lift her off the four-wheeler and said she wanted to stay right there. So Debbie wrapped her arms around her daughter and held her close, gently, not moving.

After some time, Dalia said in her sweet little bell voice, so quiet that Debbie almost missed it, "Look, Mommy, the fairies are waiting for me! I love you, Mommy!" And then she relaxed completely into Debbie's arms.

Debbie stayed still, looking for the fairies. She was surrounded by the scent of honey from the butterfly bushes, but she didn't see any fairies. She knew her little girl had gone to be with them. She softly said, "I love you, too, sweet Dalia."

Debbie sat there for a long time, hoping to freeze the moment. She held her little girl close and wished hard for things to be different.

The sun started to faintly appear in the east. She turned the four-wheeler around and headed home.

Debbie drove back slowly. She wanted to be alone with her daughter as long as she could. She didn't want to stop. She felt that if she could just ride and ride and ride, she wouldn't have to acknowledge what had just happened.

When she got home she tenderly laid Dalia back in between her stuffed toys and sat there until she heard John getting up. Even then she didn't want to shatter the moment, but knew he would want to know. She got up slowly and walked into their bedroom to tell him.

John walked into his daughter's room and lifted his little girl from the bed and cradled her in his arms. His sobs could be heard throughout the house.

The reality of Dalia's death rang in Debbie's ears.

Just at that moment the sun peeked through the window. A bright prism of purple and pink reflected off a tiny glass fairy hanging from the curtain rod and lit up the bed and Dalia's daddy. Debbie knew it was Dalia, she could feel her presence. So did John, who stopped crying and looked around as if he had just felt her touch him on his shoulder. They looked into each other's eyes and without a word, knew that Dalia was finally free.

The hospice nurse, Cindy, arrived to help where she could. She prepared a wash basin full of warm rose-scented water, and Dalia's mommy and daddy washed and dressed Dalia for the very last time. They stayed there in the room, softly talking, sharing memories, laughing, crying, and loving their little girl who had fought so courageously.

When the boys woke up, they each were given time to say goodbye and let the death of their sister settle in before anyone else was called. Their parents had prepared them and they all knew that Dalia had stayed as long as she could in this world. Robert got his favorite bunny and Josh helped him tuck it under Dalia's arm.

Cindy called the funeral home when the family was ready, and everyone said one more goodbye. They all stood in the driveway, quiet, watching the hearse disappear.

John was the first to climb onto the four-wheeler. Debbie followed, pulling Robert up to sit between them, then the older boys claimed their seats. They drove up the gravel road together, up to Dalia's favorite spot.

At the spring John turned off the motor. In silence, no one moving, they just held on to each other, all watching for a sweet little fairy with a laugh that sounded just like a fairy's bell.

One Year Later

Six weeks after Dalia died, Purple Sage was born. She holds everyone's attention with her happy, easy-going nature and sweet belly laugh. Yes, the family call her Sage, just like Dalia said they would.

Now just beginning to walk, Sage keeps her family on their toes. She has the most beautiful lavender eyes (just like her big sister), a peach complexion, and blonde, shiny hair. She is beautiful and is treasured by her family.

The boys received age-appropriate grief support through hospice, and they are doing well. I helped their school sponsor a Life Celebration for Dalia and it proved to be healing for all involved.

Josh has recently reached out to other children in his school who have also experienced loss. Because the boys may need more grief support as they develop and grow older, hospice will refer them to excellent grief counselors, if they express the need.

John went back to work and is dealing with the loss of Dalia in his own way. He feels strongly that simply by supporting his family he is doing something constructive. After reading and learning about recovering from his own grief, he does his best to support Debbie in her grieving process. They decided to schedule regular dates which are only for having fun and alone time, which John says is wonderful.

Debbie struggles with the grief of losing Dalia. She lived every day of her daughter's illness, staying with her in the hospital, holding her when she was receiving treatments, and being responsible for reducing her suffering. She wouldn't have wanted to be anywhere else. She believes mothers are supposed to make things better for their children.

But, in the end, no matter how hard she tried, she could not. When Dalia died, she was prepared, and possibly a little relieved; at least her child was no longer suffering. Dalia's death left a very big hole in her heart.

Debbie is scrapbooking their journey together and the family is still actively recounting funny and touching stories about Dalia. Debbie says, "I just want to know she won't be forgotten."

She also wants to know that her other children will be OK, so they get regular checkups. Everyone is currently very healthy.

Debbie is enjoying her growing sons, her husband, and healthy baby girl.

Hospice bereavement support is available to a family for 13 months and Debbie has accessed some of the services. I have worked with Debbie using an energy treatment called meridian tapping (page135) to help her release any lingering guilt and regret. She says after the treatment she can think of Dalia and remember the good times, more than the bad. She spends time at the bubbling spring with the wild butterfly bushes whenever she gets a chance. Debbie says every once in a while she can hear a tiny little fairy bell, and she knows Dalia is there with her.

"Life is not about waiting for the storms to pass...it's about learning how to dance in the rain."

UNKNOWN

CHAPTER 2

Leaving on Friday

Pearl was tall, lean, and tanned to the point of old leather. She lived alone in a house her husband had built in 1939. She was 97 years old and still drove her old Buick if the weather was bad, but preferred to walk.

Her home was paid for and there was little she wanted any more. She was proud of her 50 year-old, well-kept garden in the backyard that brimmed with vegetables and flowers. She fed the birds and shared her vegetables with the neighbors. She was happy and content.

When she needed help with anything she called her niece, Rebecca. So the day Pearl called Rebecca it wasn't unusual, but her request was.

Pearl announced, "Rebecca, it's time for me to go up to the hospice house because I'm dying, and I don't want to die at home, it might scare Jasper." With her next breath Pearl then asked Rebecca if she would take Jasper to live with her.

Rebecca was stunned. Pearl was her only living relative and she hadn't known her aunt to joke about important subjects. She knew Pearl was very serious if she was trying to give Jasper away. Jasper was Pearl's devoted companion, her confidant, her foot warmer, her treasured tuxedo cat.

Rebecca suggested that they first go to Pearl's doctor just in case she was mistaken. Pearl agreed but told her to get an appointment quickly because she wasn't going to wait past Friday.

Rebecca took Pearl to the doctor Monday afternoon. Her aunt had lost weight in the last 6 months and her blood test, the doctor said, did not look good. The doctor decided that, considering her age, weight and new symptoms, she qualified for hospice care. The hospice house was a great option, especially since Pearl lived alone.

Pearl moved into the hospice house Tuesday, after she made sure her neighbors would keep her garden watered and she had taken Jasper to Rebecca's home.

She was made comfortable in her new room. I came in to meet her and to take care of all the paperwork a patient has to sign before enrolling in hospice. At the hospice house we often receive patients who are acutely sick, but Pearl was different in many ways. She had driven herself to the hospice house, walked in unassisted, and was even happy to be there.

One of the many duties of my job as a social worker is to complete a personal assessment of new hospice patients and identify where they are from, how involved their family is, what their life story is, what their beliefs are, and how can we, the staff of hospice, make them as comfortable as possible. I then do my best to communicate those needs to the rest of the staff. We strive to be the support team honoring all beliefs without trying to influence or change them.

I try to establish trust as quickly as possible with anyone new. Often medical conditions can change rapidly and families can be overwhelmed. I am a guide through this process, but to do my job well I have to know who the patient is and how they are coping.

So I wanted to know how much Pearl understood what was happening to her. I wanted to know how we, the hospice staff, could reduce her anxiety and stress and how we could support and honor her individual journey. I asked Pearl if she understood where she was. Pearl told me not only where she was, but the exact address and what the field looked like before the hospice house had been built!

She was definitely alert and oriented, fully understanding everything that was going on.

Pearl told me about her life, who she knew in the community, and that years ago she had made her living as a lumber mill secretary. She told me she loved her precious cat Jasper, who was 15 years old. He was the last in a long line of big, male black-and-white tuxedo cats she had owned.

She said she was done with her life and it was time to go. "Time to go? What do you mean by that?" I asked.

Pearl replied, "Can I trust you to believe me?"

I assured her that I could be trusted, that's why I had my job. She looked at me sternly as if she was measuring what I said. Her face softened and she settled into the big comfortable chair she was sitting in, and then told me why she had come to the hospice house.

Pearl started, "Sunday morning I was tending my garden and I heard my husband calling." She smiled and continued, "I don't want to sound crazy, but that is exactly what I heard. I said, 'Yes Jim, I'm right over here,' like I had so many times before his death. Then I heard him say, 'It's time, Pearl.'"

Pearl said, "I liked to jump out of my skin when I heard that, so I left the garden and went inside where Jasper was sleeping on the couch. I walked into the kitchen and I heard another voice. This time it sounded like my sister June, and she said, 'Pearl, it's going to be fun. It's time for you to come on over and join the party.'"

After that Pearl said she poured herself a cup of coffee and sat at the kitchen table, thinking and listening for other familiar voices. She said she could hear strange conversations but couldn't make out what they were saying.

She dropped her head a little and said, "I haven't been feeling very well lately. My chest has been hurting more than normal, so Jim and

June coming for me didn't seem out of line. That's why I picked up the phone and called Rebecca."

She had told Rebecca on the way to the doctor's office about the voices. Rebecca begged her not to tell the doctor for fear they would think she was going crazy. Pearl didn't want to be crazy so she didn't tell the doctor or her nurse. Pearl said she trusted that if her husband and sister were right, she wouldn't have to talk the doctor into allowing her to go to the hospice house at all.

"I just let the facts do the talkin'." Pearl was very matter of fact with this information. I asked Pearl if she was afraid of dying.

"No," she answered. "I'm afraid of living if I can't take care of myself anymore. I think dying is going to be easy. At 97 years old I've seen most of my friends and almost all my family die, including all my children. I'm ready to go. I have no fear at all."

Pearl answered the rest of the questions I had. Our conversation ended with her telling me that a favorite treat of hers was tapioca pudding made with real eggs.

I gathered up my papers and stood up to leave. I thanked her for the lovely visit.

She said, "I'll be leaving on Friday, 'ya know. Could you come back again before that?" She obviously had enjoyed the visit. Her eyes twinkled when I said, "Of course! I'd love to know you better."

It was late Tuesday afternoon when I walked out of her room. The hospice house staff was busy making everyone comfortable and something was cooking in the oven that smelled divine. I told the nurse in charge that Pearl loved tapioca. She winked at me and said, "Then that's what she'll have tonight."

Wednesday morning I went into the hospice house just to see how everyone was and found Pearl sitting at the dining room table. She was sitting by herself looking out the window, and seemed to be talking to someone.

When I sat down across the table from her, she said in a very polite voice, "Wait a minute, Jim, that nice lady is here to talk to me again." Without skipping a beat she turned her head around and gave me her full attention.

I encouraged Pearl to talk about her life, which she was happy to do. Pearl talked about life with Jim. She told me he was a logger and she was a lumber mill secretary when they met. It was love at first sight. He was a tall drink of water with bright, laughing eyes and wavy blond hair.

She said, "Those eyes were full of love. Even when I shut my eyes today I can see them looking at me." And she took a moment and shut her eyes and smiled.

She told me that their life hadn't been easy after Jim was disabled from a tree falling on him but they got by. Pearl's eyes turned sad when she talked about her children.

"We had four beautiful babies. The first one was a healthy boy. The last three were little girls, but they each died within a few hours after being born. Those were the hard years. I thought I was doing something wrong but in the end, after talking to a lot of doctors, Jim and I discovered it was because of the Rh factor."

Pearl stopped for a moment and took a deep breath. "I never got over losing those sweet babies, but after I found out it wasn't my fault, I stopped grieving so hard."

She said their son Kenny was their delight. "We raised him in the mountains and he grew to be a big, strapping kid who looked just like Jim, and he became a logger like his dad." She took a shuddering breath and continued, "When he turned 19 he was drafted. Just before his 20th birthday he was killed in Vietnam." Pearl's eyes filled with tears retelling Kenny's story, and she took a moment to gather herself again.

We talked about Pearl's beliefs. She was a religious woman and had regularly gone to church. She said she wasn't set on just one religion, so she often visited different churches in her community. She believed she had been the best person she could be--not perfect, but good enough.

15

At that point in the conversation Rebecca arrived to visit her aunt. I then excused myself, since Pearl became focused on how Jasper was doing and how efficiently Rebecca was watering her garden.

Thursday afternoon I returned to the hospice house. The hospice nurse said that Pearl had not eaten since last night and had spent the whole day in bed.

She said, "Pearl just doesn't have the spark she came into the hospice house with." The nurse was surprised at Pearl's sudden decline. Shaking her head, she said, "It looks like she is starting her dying process."

When I got to Pearl's room, Rebecca was sitting on the couch, quietly knitting. The lights were dim. Pearl appeared pale and tiny in the big hospital bed. She was having another conversation with someone unseen.

Pearl said, "Mama, I was hopin' to see Pa with you. Yes, I am coming, but I'm not sure how I'm supposed to get there."

Rebecca turned to me and said, "She's been like this all day, talking to her dead relatives, apparently making plans, then talking to me in the same breath."

Just then Pearl said, "Oh, that nice gal is back to see me. If you don't mind I want to visit with her a little." Pearl turned her head and looked right at me.

I asked Pearl if she was comfortable. She quietly replied, "I'm having a little pain in my side but nothing I need medication for."

I asked her who she was visiting with and she reported that she was seeing family long gone.

Her eyes still had a tiny bit of twinkle left. I sat and talked with Pearl and Rebecca, encouraging Rebecca to talk about any unfinished business that might need to be addressed. It was obvious something was happening. Pearl didn't have much more time.

I asked Rebecca if she wanted to tell her aunt goodbye. Rebecca looked at me as if I had been drinking whatever her aunt was drinking. She asked if I was serious. I agreed that her aunt's reaction was very unusual, but her nurses and I were seeing signs of rapid decline. At that moment Rebecca realized that her Aunt Pearl could very well be dying, just like she said she would.

Rebecca tearfully told her aunt that she loved her and would really miss her. She reminded Pearl what an amazing friend and aunt she had been.

Pearl quipped, "And because he was mine, you'll love Jasper forever, too." We all laughed.

I encouraged Pearl to talk about what was happening to her, but she really seemed to be living in two worlds and became irritated with my questioning.

She said, "It is what it is; I can't explain it clearer than that."

Pearl was comfortable and knew she was loved by her dear Rebecca. I left the room, not knowing how Pearl would fare through the night.

Friday morning first thing I drove to the hospice house. I walked down to Pearl's room and found two devoted nurses standing beside her bed. They were holding Pearl's hands, stroking her hair, telling her it would be OK. She was breathing her last.

I asked if Rebecca had been called and they both nodded. She raced down the hall a minute later. As she arrived she said tearfully, "I love you, Auntie Pearl!" And then Pearl's last breath was expelled.

We were all stunned. Pearl had done exactly what she said she would do. Rebecca was tearful but let out a short laugh.

She said, "My Aunt Pearl always was a character and a woman of her word, right down to the last day of her life."

Four Months Later

Rebecca, the last living relative, inherited Pearl's estate and happily moved into the old family home. The garden will be continued next spring in Pearl's memory and shared with all the neighbors.

Jasper is back to his spot on the couch, happy in his cat routine. Rebecca enjoys his cranky old cat company and says she does love him, most of the time.

Because Rebecca experienced the dying process with her Aunt Pearl she did not require any grief support. It's available to her, but she tells me that she's not sad. She is grateful she had Pearl in her life as long as she did and is content and happy. Rebecca says she hopes one day Pearl will call for her.

"Just," she adds, "hopefully not before my 97th birthday!"

Of all existing things

some are in our power,

and others are not in our power.

In our power are thought,

impulse,

will to get and will to avoid,

in a few words,

everything which is our own doing…

What disturbs men's minds

is not events

but their judgments on events…

Ask not that events should happen as you will,

but let your will be that events

should happen as they do,

and you shall have peace.

EPICTETUS

You have got to own your days and name them, each one of them,
or else the years go right by and none of them belong to you.

HERB GARDNER
A THOUSAND CLOWNS

CHAPTER 3

Carrots, Eggs, and Coffee

A young woman went to her mother and told her about her life and how things were so hard for her. She did not know how she was going to make it and wanted to give up. She was tired of fighting and struggling. It seemed as one problem was solved, a new one would arise.

Her mother took her to the kitchen. She filled three pots with water and placed each on a high fire. Soon the pots came to boil. In the first she placed carrots, in the second she placed eggs, and in the last she placed ground coffee beans. Without saying a word, she let them sit and boil.

In about twenty minutes she turned off the burners. She fished the carrots out and placed them in a bowl. She pulled the eggs out and placed them in a bowl. Then she ladled the coffee out and placed it in a bowl. Turning to her daughter, she asked, "Tell me what you see."

"Carrots, eggs, and coffee," her daughter replied.

Her mother brought her closer and asked her to feel the carrots. She did and noted that they were soft. The mother then asked the daughter to take an egg and break it. After peeling off the shell, she felt the hardboiled egg.

Finally, the mother asked the daughter to sip the coffee. The daughter smiled as she tasted its richness. The daughter then asked, 'What does it mean, mother?'

Her mother explained that each of these objects had faced the same adversity—boiling water—but each had reacted differently.

The carrot went in strong, hard, and unrelenting. However, after being subjected to the boiling water, it softened and became weak.

The egg had been fragile. Its thin outer shell had protected its liquid interior, but after sitting in the boiling water, its inside became hardened.

The ground coffee beans were unique, however. After they were in the boiling water, they changed the water.

Turning to her daughter, she asked, "Which are you? When adversity knocks on your door, how do you respond? Are you a carrot, an egg or a coffee bean?"

So consider this: which are you? Are you the carrot that seems strong, but with pain and adversity you wilt and become soft and lose your strength?

Are you the egg that starts with a liquid heart, but changes with the heat? Did you have a fluid spirit, but after a death, a breakup, a financial hardship or some other trial, become hardened and stiff? Does your shell look the same, but on the inside, are you bitter and tough, with a stiff spirit and hardened heart?

Or are you like the coffee bean? The bean actually changes the hot water, the very circumstance that brings the pain. When the water gets hot, it releases its fragrance and flavor. If you are like the bean, when things are at their worst, you get better and change the situation around you.

When the hour is darkest and trials are at their greatest, do you elevate yourself to another level? How do you handle adversity? Are you a carrot, an egg or a coffee bean?

May you have enough happiness to make you sweet, enough trials to make you strong, enough sorrow to keep you human and enough hope to make you happy.

The happiest of people don't necessarily have the best of everything; they just make the most of everything that comes their way. The brightest future will always be based on a forgotten past. You can't go forward in life until you let go of your past failures and heartaches.

When you were born, you were crying and everyone around you was smiling. Live your life so at the end, you're the one who is smiling and everyone around you is crying.

AUTHOR UNKNOWN

The best and most beautiful things in the world cannot be seen or even touched. They must be felt with the heart.

HELEN KELLER

CHAPTER 4

When Someone Cares

Louie was a sweet, jovial man, 89 years old. He claimed he was 5'4"
but for all intents and purposes his stocky body stood barely five feet
tall. His true lifelong passion was his relationship with his lovely wife,
Gina. She had died ten years ago. After that, Louie pretty much lost
interest in keeping his house up or caring for himself, so he moved into
a graduated care facility. The care facility had been Louie's home for
the past 9 years.

The facility was not the highest quality operation but it was all Louie
could afford. The cost of living there used up almost all of his Social
Security benefits, less $35 a month he could use for incidentals. Gina's
illness before her death had decimated their small "rainy day" savings.

"This place is OK," he said, "I don't need more and I don't want
less."

He had made a few friends at the place, but no one visited him from
outside the facility. When Gina died, she was his last living relative.

The hospice nurse, Jillian, and I met Louie when he was sitting in
the barber's chair. He was getting his "tender young hairs trimmed," he
said with a definite Scottish brogue. He greeted me with a joke about
his shiny head. Louie said he believed that if he took really good care

of his wispy hair he'd be able to court his wife again when he finally got to heaven.

His smile was wide, but the beads of sweat on his white upper lip revealed he was in a lot of pain. He didn't know it, but Jillian and I were already assessing him. We could see he was not comfortable. He was trying to hide his discomfort with humor, but his pain showed clearly on his face.

When his haircut was finished, we walked back to his room. His steps were cautious and slow and he told me his days weren't so good anymore.

As we entered his room, Jillian asked what level of pain he was experiencing, measuring it with a 1 being nothing much to 10 being unbearable.

He gently said, "10 would be doable. I'm not sure if my pain is a 15 or a 20, but I can tell you if I was a screaming man, I would be breaking your eardrums."

Jillian was very concerned with that description and asked Louie what kind of medication he was taking for the pain.

Louie responded, "The nurse gives me a little white pill and a big blue pill in the evening, and that seems to help me sleep but I don't think I get anything for my back pain."

Jillian excused herself and went off to find the care facility nurse to try and determine what medication Louie could have to relieve his pain.

We had been visiting with Louie less than twenty minutes when we discovered he was dealing with terrible pain, and had very little relief from it. Louie's pain, we suspected, was from his bones, a common complication of prostate cancer. He had been diagnosed three years ago. His doctor had told him he would probably die from something else before the cancer would kill him. Unfortunately, his prostate cancer had other ideas, and now it had already spread to his spine.

While Jillian was trying to find out if Louie had pain medication, I continued the visit to see if he wanted hospice support. I explained that the doctor sent us because he believed that the prostate cancer had progressed so far as to be life-limiting. I told him that hospice is a support team, a team of professionals designed to advocate for his needs and help him reduce his pain and other symptoms. I emphasized that it would be *his* team, one that would be focused on supporting his way of life, using his ideals. He was worried about trying to pay for the added support but when I explained that Medicare paid for it, he signed up. After all the initial paperwork was done, I had a chance to get to know him.

Louie was originally from Scotland and moved to Canada when he was 19 years old. He enlisted in the Canadian Army and fought in World War II, "Alongside you Yanks," he said, grinning.

He was stationed in Italy. Louie said he loved the local people, the food and the language. He said, "I even took classes to learn to speak Italian. I wanted to be able to talk to them." He winked and said, "I discovered a very good reason to communicate in Italian."

Louie went on to tell me that as a young soldier he never missed the USO dances that were held on the base once a month for the servicemen.

"I can still hear the big band playing," Louie reminisced, "and see all those pretty girls just looking for a dance partner. I was in heaven." And he looked away with a far off gaze.

He said, "That's where I met my sweet Gina. The first time I saw her I knew she would be my wife."

Louie then sat up straight and said, "In my best 'Italiano' I asked her to dance." He smiled, remembering his excitement, "The next week I met her family, and I asked her father for her hand in marriage!" Louie laughed. "Those were the days!"

Jillian returned with a pill and a frustrated look on her face. She said, "You have a mild pain reliever prescribed but nothing that will help you with the pain you are describing."

Jillian explained that she would talk to Louie's doctor and advocate for him to have more effective pain medication.

Louie said, "Honestly, I haven't wanted to bother the doctor with my problems--he is such a busy guy." "But" he added, "I sure would appreciate some help with my pain."

Jillian told Louie that by the end of the day she would have more appropriate medication for him.

Louie stood up and hugged us both, thanking us for our time. He chose to stay in his room 'to catch a little nap' as he put it, but we all knew it was just too painful for him to walk us to the door.

After a few visits I came to know Louie much better. He was always honest about how he was doing. He would remind me at each appointment that he wasn't sure if he believed in a higher power, but said he prayed every night he would die, anyway.

"I'm done," he would say, "I'm tired of the pain."

Jillian was working with Louie's doctor to help control Louie's pain. The doctor had prescribed effective pain medication, but because of where Louie lived, his medication was not always properly given and sometimes even forgotten. Louie's care facility didn't have the staff or the requirements to give him his medications on time.

Louie seemed to enjoy my visits and shared with me what he called "the important parts of my life." He told me that he and Gina married at the end of the war and immigrated to the United States. After a year of married bliss, Zita, their beautiful baby daughter, arrived. Two years later, they were blessed with Sophia.

Louie said, "They looked just like Gina, beautiful silky, dark brown hair and big brown eyes." He lamented, "I was the happiest I had ever been when my family was all together."

Louie tearfully told me about his little girls. He said, "We lived in upstate New York. I had a job working in a mill and couldn't buy my girls everything they wanted." He smiled, "But they didn't ask for much, either. They loved to swim and play outside, go for rides on their bicycles and laugh. Oh, how they could laugh!" And he stopped for a minute, as if listening to the sound of his two little girls laughing.

He added, "When the girls were eleven and nine, Gina discovered they could go to a summer camp right down the road. Because we were neighbors and the girls were still pretty young, they could go to the camp all day and then come home at night. It didn't cost very much. Gina was even able to enjoy the camp with them when she wanted to."

He continued, "One very hot day Zita went swimming in the camp lake. That in itself was not unusual, but this day she went with older girls." Louie's voice got noticeably quieter.

"They decided to swim out to the floating dock in the middle of the lake. Zita was 11 and probably thought she could do anything the older girls could do. But Zita wasn't a strong swimmer, and unnoticed by the older girls, she quickly got into trouble."

Louie took another breath and said, "Sophia apparently had been watching her older sister and realized she was struggling. Instead of calling out for help," Louie spoke grimly, "she tried to swim out to help her big sister."

Louie whispered, "We lost both our little girls that day. That was the day our world came crashing down."

Louie said it still broke his heart to tell that story, even 60 years later. He said, "We decided not to have any more children after that. I'm not sure if it was a good decision, but it was our decision and we lived with it."

Louie looked at me when he was finished and said, "You just never know, do you? Kiss and love your family every day, 'cause you just never know."

He grieved, "I lost Gina ten years ago and I can't say that I've gotten over her death. But when she died, I can honestly say she knew I loved her. I tried to give her the best life I could." He looked up at me and said, "Even today I'd still like to tell her, 'Gina, I love you,' just one more time."

On one visit, instead of meeting me in the foyer, which was Louie's habit, the staff told me he was in bed and hadn't been up all day. I went to his room and found him lying in his hospital bed, staring at the ceiling. He smiled when I entered. Observing his pale complexion and the beads of perspiration on his forehead, I could tell his pain was once again out of control.

I called Jillian, and asked her to come out as soon as possible. Then I stomped down to the medical station and demanded to know when Louie had last been given his pain medication. The medical aide sitting behind the glass window was reading a romance novel. She looked up unimpressed and said, "Oh, we were just on our way to give Louie his meds."

I was indignant. I hate to see someone in pain because of incompetency. I asked to see his medication schedule. The medical aide gave it to me and walked away.

It had clearly and painstakingly been documented by Jillian as to what, how much, and when Louie's medication was supposed to be given. The medical aide, Linda, had missed giving Louie his medication by nearly an hour.

To her credit, Linda did hurry down to Louie's room and administer his pain medication. She became tearful when she saw how much pain he was in.

She said, "When I gave Louie his medication four hours ago he didn't even seem to need it. I didn't think a few minutes would make any difference."

Then she said, with heartfelt emotion, "Louie, I am so sorry. I promise when I'm on duty I will never let you go without your medicine again."

Louie gave her a painful smile and said, "I'll hold you to that promise, young lady." Then Linda left the room.

When Louie's pain was under control he wanted to visit again. Louie didn't have much money because all his money went to his care, so his next statement caught me off guard.

Louie said, "Well, lassie, why don't you and I blow this place for a while and get a couple of drinks!" He took my hand and, seeing my wedding ring said, "As a matter of fact, he can come, too."

I asked him where he had in mind and he said, "Anywhere but here!" But when he looked at me, we both knew getting him out of bed was just not an option.

I suggested that instead of "blowing this place" and because it was so close to Christmas, I would read a special book I had brought called *The Polar Express*. We had talked about the book at my last visit and he was excited to hear more. He settled down in his hospital bed, shut his eyes and intently listened as I read. Sometimes his eyes would pop open at a particularly exciting part. But most of the time they were tightly shut.

At the end of the story Louie looked like a little boy, his eyes sparkling with possibilities. He said excitedly, "I'm sure that story was written about me. I've always believed in Santa Claus and I know I can hear Santa's sleigh bells even now!"

When I left him that afternoon he was falling asleep, murmuring about trains, snow and holes in his pockets. I left the book on the table beside his bed. I thought if he woke up he might want to look through its wonderful pictures.

I visited every other day after that. I could see he was rapidly declining, and being in a big facility without family visiting, he needed someone to advocate for him. Linda, the facility medication nurse, true to her word did medicate him on time when she was there, but she only worked three days a week. But her promise was passed on though the staff, and now all the medical aides were making a point to medicate Louie on time.

One time when I was visiting Louie, I noticed he was cold to the touch even though he was completely covered up in his hospital bed. He was wide awake and shivering. Louie told me he wasn't wearing any pajamas--not by his choice, but because the aides had told him it was just easier to keep him clean.

He complained, "They forget that I'm a skinny old man and need my drawers on to keep warm."

I asked him if he wanted some help getting his pajamas on, and he said, "Yes, it would be a great favor to me and my dignity."

I asked an aide who was tidying up Louie's room if she would help him get his pajamas on. She glared at me and said, "The orders from the director are to only put adult briefs on Louie because it's too hard to undress him."

I asked the aide to please get Linda. I knew Linda had a soft spot in her heart for Louie, and would probably help. The aide left, but after 30 minutes it seemed she wasn't on her intended errand, and Louie was still shivering. He looked at me expectantly, raised his eyebrows, and said, "I'm game if you are!" He chuckled at the thought of me helping him into his pajamas.

He pointed to his flannels lying on top of the chest of drawers and looked at me. "What do you think, lassie? I'm freezing under here!"

He let out a laugh and clapped his cold hands together when he saw me reach for his flannel pajamas.

He said, "I knew you'd come through for me!"

Dressing a patient is not a hospice social worker's job, but I knew that without my help it might not happen. Honoring Louie's wishes and maintaining his dignity was part of my job, and this was what he was requesting.

32

Louie was stiff, cold and very weak, but he helped when he could. He struggled to sit up, and I struggled to get the flannel pajama top on him with the least amount of pain. Moving did hurt him, but even when he yelled out in pain, he followed it with encouragement and gentle chuckles.

The pajama top was a piece of cake in contrast to the bottoms. Louie couldn't stand up so they had to be put on one leg at a time. After some maneuvering and stopping to laugh a little, Louie and I discovered a minor miscalculation; he couldn't lift himself up. I couldn't get his pants all the way up to his waist.

Louie laughed and said, "Well I can't very well meet my maker with my drawers half way down, now, can I? Gina will be wanting to know what I was up to!"

He had a twinkle in his eye and seemed to be thoroughly enjoying himself. I, on the other hand, was a bit worried about what to do next.

The door opened and Linda walked into the room. She said, "You called?" and grinned at both of us.

I stepped away from the hospital bed and she immediately saw the predicament.

Louie couldn't control his amusement, and he pointed at me and said, "Really, it's all her fault!"

Linda laughed and said, "I'll bet!" and winked at me. "Get on the other side of the bed. Together we can get those pajama pants where they are supposed to be!"

Louie was thrilled with the help and finally warm. He looked positively regal in his Scottish, black watch patterned pajamas.

Linda gave Louie his medication. When he was comfortable, he asked me to read *The Polar Express* again. This time he asked Linda to sit down with us and shut her eyes. She had time, so she did just that. Louie sat watching Linda's face. When her expression changed, Louie's expression mirrored hers. I left his room with the two of them looking at the pictures and talking about whether they could hear sleigh bells or not.

The last time I had the pleasure of Louie's company, I walked into his room to see him staring at three different kinds of pudding on his bed tray. He loved pudding, but couldn't eat it any longer. He was too weak.

Linda and a few other staff members had made a point of giving him a lot of tender loving care. He was wearing dark red flannel pajamas and looked cozy and content. We talked about where he was going. He was looking forward to the 'trip'. He was planning on going over to the Other Side on a big steel train steaming into the night.

He said, "I know my Gina is waiting for me at the next stop, and maybe Zita and Sophia will be there, too."

He was weak and kept falling asleep, but asked me to read *The Polar Express* once more. I started to read it when the door to his room opened. Two aides I hadn't met before came in. One whispered to the other, "You've got to shut your eyes."

Before I knew it, six aides were sitting in the room with us, all with their eyes closed, listening intently to the story. When I was done, Louie was sound asleep. The aides quietly discussed whether they could hear the sleigh bells or not. Louie's room was warm and full of laughter, and that's exactly what he would have wanted.

The next day Louie no longer responded. When I visited, Linda was sitting beside him reading the story. A few aides—Louie's new friends--were in the room, all with their eyes closed, listening intently. They opened their eyes to acknowledge my presence but then looked expectantly at Linda to finish her task.

Louie died later that evening. Linda said he quietly slipped away somewhere in the middle of the story. She said no one noticed because they had all had their eyes shut.

Louie probably just got on the Polar Express when it stopped. He was ready and knew his family was waiting.

Epilogue

Louie was cremated by the county. He didn't have any known relatives. No one claimed his ashes. They were eventually buried by the county.

We all deserve dignity and respect, especially when we are vulnerable and dying. The act of putting on Louie's pajamas was a way of honoring him and supporting his dignity.

Because hospice was involved, Louie became the focus of care rather than a chore. Before he died, he knew someone cared.

A friend is someone who knows the song in your heart and can sing it back to you when you have forgotten the words.

UNKNOWN

CHAPTER 5

The Kindness of Strangers

Christy was 37 and a single mother of two daughters. She had long black hair, a pale complexion, and stood about 6 feet tall. She was thin and willowy and had eyes like dark meadow pools, green and mysterious. She had been a model in her early 20s. From her high cheek bones and beautiful smile it was easy to see why.

Christy arrived in town after a 14 hour Greyhound bus ride. She had started her trip at Huntington Beach with her 4 year old daughter, Natalie, by her side. She had left her 16 year old daughter with friends. The new tumor growing between her shoulder blades made it impossible for Christy to lay back and rest in the bus seat.

She sat forward the whole trip, rocking with her eyes shut and remembering her best friend Andrea's words, "Please come, Christy, I can help you with Natalie and I can help you get treatment. Together we can beat this cancer. I'm here for you. You can stay with me until you get better. We've been friends since kindergarten, you can count on me."

Christy was desperate. There was no one else who could help her. She was confident she would find unconditional love and friendship at the end of the ride. Even though they hadn't seen each other in years,

Andrea and Christy had kept in touch by phone and Christmas cards for more than 20 years. Christy was excited to finally see her dear high school friend and meet the rest of Andrea's family. She didn't know if she would like living in a small town, but she was willing to give it a try, especially since Andrea would be there.

Natalie slept most of the way or quietly played with her dolls. The little bit of food Christy packed lasted for only the first half of the trip, but she wasn't worried. She knew Andrea would be there to meet them. Her own pain made it impossible for her to have any kind of appetite.

When the bus finally pulled into Andrea's town, Christy and her daughter looked out the window, hoping for a quick peek of Andrea before they got off. But they didn't see her.

Natalie whined to her mother, "I'm hungry!" and Christy said they would eat in just a little while. They climbed off the bus, gathered their luggage and looked around.

No one was waiting at the bus stop.

Christy was stunned. She knew Andrea was expecting her. She sat with Natalie on the bench and waited. After a while Christy called Andrea. The answering machine was on; she could only leave a message. By now they were both exhausted. Still, there was no Andrea, so Christy decided to look for a place to eat.

They got up and dragged their luggage down the street. Before she had walked a block they came face to face with an elderly couple. The man asked if she needed help carrying her luggage. With Natalie in tears, this kind gesture overcame Christy and she burst into tears, too.

The couple introduced themselves and after hearing about Christy's plight, said they didn't live far and would be glad to take them to their home and feed them. Christy agreed, and was thankful for her newfound friends, Ron and Patti.

Patti made a grilled cheese sandwich for Natalie. Christy was able to lie on their couch and get some badly needed rest from the pain shooting through her body. Before she knew it, she awoke with a start. Darkness was falling.

Across the room she could see Natalie sitting on Patti's lap. They were reading a children's book. Natalie looked freshly bathed and was wearing her pink pajamas. She was obviously enjoying herself. Christy sighed with relief.

Ron noticed she was awake and offered her something to drink and a bite to eat. She couldn't believe how sweet these strangers were and emotion choked her again. Ron told Christy that with the information she had given him, he had discovered where Andrea worked in town. He revealed that Andrea's reaction was surprise at Christy being in town.

Christy was shocked with that news and hoped Ron had misunderstood Andrea's reaction. She asked if Andrea had mentioned when she would be coming to get them.

Ron, almost too quiet for Christy to hear, said, "Andrea said she'd pick you up tomorrow." Christy was dumbfounded.

Ron and Patti invited the two to stay the night. Christy didn't want to impose, but they were so nice and her money so limited she accepted. That night she and Natalie both slept like babies. Ron and Patti treated Christy like she had hoped Andrea would, and Natalie enjoyed all the extra attention.

The next morning Andrea arrived and greeted Christy and Natalie. She didn't have any explanation as to why she hadn't been at the bus station to meet them. Christy was so relieved to see Andrea she didn't question her. Ron and Patti again mentioned they would be glad to help in any way. After exchanging goodbyes they were off in Andrea's car.

Christy tried to have a casual conversation with her friend but Andrea seemed preoccupied. Maybe it was because I don't look healthy, Christy thought.

In fact, her tumors made her look so lumpy it seemed like she had swallowed different sized ball-bearings. Some were the size of a pea and others were the size of a golf ball, all protruding and quite visible. Some were dark brown and the newer ones were red and purple. They were on her face, back, chest and legs. The red ones hurt all the time.

Tears ran down Christy's face when she thought about how she looked and the fear that her friend, her dear friend, wasn't prepared for the reality of her disease.

Christy sat quietly beside Andrea, hoping she would say something. Eventually she did talk but was distant, and acted more like Christy and Natalie were an annoyance.

She told Christy she hadn't told her husband they were coming. Andrea said as soon as she had a chance to talk to her husband and he agreed, they might be able to move in with them.

Christy didn't know what to do if Andrea didn't take her in. She didn't even know where she was headed, let alone how she could survive without the help Andrea promised.

She quickly wiped away her tears and busied herself with encouraging Natalie to look out at the forest they were driving through.

After about 30 miles they arrived at a little cabin. Andrea stopped the car and got out. As she unloaded groceries she pointed towards the river which was down a steep slope behind the cabin.

"There are bears that fish in that river; don't go down without a big stick," she laughed as she walked to the cabin.

Christy and Natalie got out cautiously and stretched, taking in their forest surroundings. Natalie, a little scared, held her mother's hand and looked around with big eyes.

Christy called to Andrea, "You're kidding, right?" But Andrea didn't answer. She just hunched her shoulders and set her lips, as if to say, it's not my problem.

Andrea unlocked the door to the cabin. It was dark inside and smelled a little musty but it was fully furnished and had electricity. Once they unloaded Christy's luggage and the groceries Andrea had bought and turned on the lights, the interior brightened.

It was a small one room cabin. An antique four poster bed sat in the middle of the living room. A wood stove was tucked into the corner with a rocking chair beside it. Behind a curtain at the back of the room was a simple kitchen and bathroom. Andrea proudly told Christy she had rented the cabin for a short while until she could get things organized at her home.

Christy, caught off guard at this turn of events and exhausted from all her travels, was just grateful to have a place to call her own for a while. She asked Andrea how long it would be before she and Natalie could move into her home.

Andrea stopped, looked straight at Christy and said, "Who's to say, but for now you'll be staying here." Taken aback by her friend's brusque answer, Christy didn't reply.

Andrea busied herself in the kitchen and made dinner. It was an old favorite from their childhood days, spaghetti and meat balls. Even though she didn't feel like eating, Christy tried. When they were finished with dinner, Andrea cleaned up, gathered up her jacket and purse and said she would be back.

Christy asked, "When?"

Andrea nonchalantly said, "As soon as I can, just trust me." Then she got in her car and left.

Christy felt a little panic rise up in her throat when she realized she and her daughter were all alone and she had no idea where they were. Bears walking around near the river flashed through her mind. She quickly locked the cabin door, hoping it was strong enough to keep out the wild animals.

Feeling scared, she turned around and saw Natalie staring at her. The four year old did not realize that this was not the plan Christy had in mind. All Natalie wanted was a bedtime story and her mommy to tuck her in.

The pain from her tumors intensified with movement but Christy helped Natalie get into her pink pajamas anyway. Fishing through their luggage Natalie found the book Patti had given her. It was *Clifford's Good Deeds,* by Norman Bridwell.

With the book under her arm the little girl climbed into the big four poster bed. Christy climbed in after her. She just couldn't face the pain it would cost her to get undressed. They both fell asleep with all the lights on, happy to be together.

In the morning Christy discovered a beautiful view of the river from the kitchen window. She looked in the refrigerator and found the leftover spaghetti, a half gallon of milk, a dozen eggs, a package of cheddar cheese, a loaf of bread and some pickles. She found some cereal in the cupboards, along with a few crackers and a bag of almonds. It was only enough food for a couple of days but she wasn't worried. Andrea would surely be back by the afternoon.

After Christy made breakfast and Natalie ate every last bite, Christy thought how nice a hot shower would feel. She had Natalie sit in the sun that was streaming through the window and encouraged her to play with her dolls. She busied herself brushing her teeth while she waited for the water to warm up.

Five minutes later it was still as ice cold as when she turned it on. She put her robe back on, looked at Natalie playing in the sunshine, and tried to decide what to do.

She decided to look for the hot water heater, thinking maybe it hadn't been turned on, but after a quick search discovered there wasn't one.

Trying not to fall apart in front of her little girl, she put a pan of water on the stove and heated it.

Christy washed herself standing naked in the kitchen. She had to move carefully and slowly; every movement caused pain. Her tumors were tender and she wasn't always aware where a new one was developing.

When she finished, she was cold and exhausted. She put her robe back on and barely made it back into bed. Lying there, staring at the ceiling, she fell into a deep sleep.

All of a sudden she was startled by Natalie shaking her, crying that she was scared and hungry. Christy realized she had slept most of the day and now it was almost dark. The cabin was freezing.

She forced herself to get up and be attentive to Natalie. Christy made eggs and toast for dinner. Natalie ate her meal and Christy ate a few bites but felt nauseous and decided not to push her luck.

She put a pan of water on the stove to heat for Natalie's bath, but the activity proved too difficult, forcing Christy to lie down again. Natalie tried to get her mother to read to her, but Christy fell asleep. Natalie fell asleep beside her. All the lights were on in the cabin again, but no one noticed.

The next morning Christy realized she was in a terrible situation. She didn't know where she was, didn't have a telephone and didn't have any transportation.

She started to worry that Andrea might not come back. Her anxiety quickly turned to fear. She decided to try to find help by walking back to the main road.

Christy helped Natalie get her coat on and they started down the long driveway toward the main road. But Christy's pain increased and the two didn't get far before they turned back to the cabin.

With great effort Christy made another meal and then had to lay back down, exhausted. She read aloud to Natalie from her new book. It was all she could do.

They spent the day either in bed or sitting in the rocking chair, a constant feeling of exhaustion pulling at Christy. Often sleep overwhelmed her until she would wake with a start, making sure Natalie was safe.

Andrea drove down the driveway on the afternoon of the third day.

When Christy didn't open the door to greet her, she knocked. Natalie opened the door and started crying hysterically, pointing at her mother lying face down on the bed. Andrea was shocked and rushed to Christy. She was alive but groaned loudly when Andrea shook her.

Andrea called out, "Christy, oh my God! Christy, are you ok?"

Christy turned on to her side slowly and glared out from under the dark hair that lay across her face. She could hear Natalie sobbing at the end of the bed. Christy was honestly relieved to see Andrea but furious that her so-called friend had left her in the woods without help.

She spat out, "What the f**k were you thinking, leaving us out here, you heartless bitch! If you didn't want me to come, why did you ask me?"

She was crying now, and her back hurt with every word. "I can barely stand! I'm so sick I can't eat! You just left us! You didn't care! You left us, you miserable bitch!" Then Christy realized how upset her yelling made Natalie and held her arms out to her.

As Natalie crawled into her arms, she said, "My sweet little girl, you are so brave, I'm so sorry mommy was yelling. You are such a good girl! Mommy loves you more than anything! Now that Andrea is here everything is going to be fine. You are such a brave good girl," she cooed to her daughter.

Natalie looked up at her mother, blinking her tears away, reassured by her soothing voice.

Andrea looked around the cabin and saw evidence of what had happened during the past three days. The room was in total disarray. Clothes were spilled everywhere, and most of the bedding was on the floor. Spaghetti had hardened on the rocking chair and the pan lay on the floor.

Christy, in obvious pain, said weakly, "Andrea, I need to go to a doctor today. I am completely out of pain medication and I can't eat anything without vomiting. I need to find better living arrangements for Natalie and me."

Andrea, feeling offended, replied, "Well, I can't take you to my house yet. I brought food out so you and Natalie can stay here a little longer until my husband decides if he wants to take you and your kid on."

Christy looked at her friend and said, slowly and evenly, "You will take Natalie and me into town today, and you will take me to a doctor or a clinic or a hospital, somewhere I can get some help with my pain."

Andrea knew she meant business. Avoiding Christy's stare, she started gathering their belongings.

They stumbled out to the car, Christy hanging onto Andrea, the pain almost too much to bear. Natalie sat in the back with her mother, scared and crying.

During the ride Andrea announced, "I think you should go to the hospital, we don't have clinics like big towns and I don't know any doctors." She glanced in the rearview mirror and saw Christy just nod at the idea.

Andrea drove the rest of the 30 miles back to town without another word. She drove straight to the emergency room and helped Christy in. Natalie followed, carrying her mother's purse.

After checking in, the nurse came out with a wheelchair and helped Christy into it. After telling the little girl to stay with Andrea while she helped her mommy, the nurse looked up.

Andrea was gone.

Natalie followed the nurse and her mother into the emergency room. Christy was helped onto a gurney. The ER doctor told Christy that, considering her condition, she needed to be admitted to the hospital right away.

Christy asked to use a phone. She dialed Ron and Patti's number. She hoped they were telling the truth when they told her to call if she needed anything.

Patti answered, and Christy started crying. She told Patti where she was and Patti said she would be right there.

Patti was allowed into the emergency room even through she wasn't family. When Natalie spotted her, she ran to the older woman. Patti bent down to Natalie and the child buried her face in Patti's shoulder. She sat holding her, speaking soothing words to her, trying to calm her. When Natalie finally calmed down she fell asleep in Patti's arms and then the women had a chance to talk.

Christy told Patti of the cabin experience and her fear of dying out in the middle of nowhere, without a way to get help for Natalie. She said she could no longer trust Andrea and had to find some place safe for Natalie or she could not stay in the hospital. Patti volunteered to take Natalie until Christy was back on her feet.

Christy had no other choice. She realized Patti was almost a complete stranger but had shown more compassion and love than she had known for a long time.

Patti gently woke Natalie up and told her she was going to go home with her until her mommy felt better. Natalie started crying again.

Exhausted and scared, Natalie cried, "But we forgot my Clifford book at the cabin!"

Patti assured her that she had other books at her home that Natalie was sure to like. Armed with that information Natalie said, "Mommy, I can go with Patti, she has good books to read to me. I love you, Mommy," and stood bravely beside Patti, holding her hand.

Patti assured Christy she was welcome to call them anytime, and that Patti would call her at the hospital, too. She would also bring Natalie in to see Christy every day until she was better.

It was Christy's turn to cry as she watched her little girl and this wonderful lady walk out of the emergency room.

The doctors called for all of Christy's medical records at Huntington Beach and did a few tests of their own. She stayed in the hospital for five long days. Her pain was better controlled but her appetite was very poor.

When the doctor arrived to talk to her about the tests results he looked pretty grim. The news wasn't what Christy expected. She knew she had cancer and that the tumors were increasing, but she didn't think she was going to die soon.

The doctor was clear--the medical tests showed tumors all over her body, not just on the outside. They were inside, too, involving her liver and possibly her brain. He did not expect her to live more than six more months.

When Christy heard she was dying, she stopped listening to the doctor. He kindly suggested hospice but she just saw his lips moving. 'Six months or less' repeated in her mind. "Six months or less! What about my girls?" agonized Christy.

Talking to Sandy was the first thing she thought about. Sandy was her 16 year old daughter who was still living in Huntington Beach. She was living with her best friend from school, Megan.

When Megan's parents, Frank and Judy, heard that Christy was moving up north, they asked if Sandy could stay with them. It was a generous offer; one Christy encouraged Sandy to accept. It meant Sandy could stay in school and live with a nice family, a real family who could give Sandy what Christy couldn't.

Before she left, Frank and Judy had guardian papers drawn up, and Christy signed them. She was grateful Sandy would have the experience of a stable family who would treat her as if she was their own daughter.

Christy realized, lying in the hospital bed, that she hadn't really said goodbye to her daughter before leaving town. Sandy wasn't home when Christy called so she left a message on her daughter's voice mail.

She felt a pang of regret and guilt. She said quietly to herself, "I could have tried harder." She sighed and shut her eyes, a tear rolling down her cheek.

She thought about Sandy's life.

It hadn't been easy. Her father abandoned them when Sandy was about two years old. Christy had struggled to make ends meet. Then the drugs started.

Christy got involved with methamphetamine, and the dark world that surrounds it. As Sandy got older she started seeking refuge with the families of her friends from school. It made sense that she was with Megan's family now.

She decided to call Sandy again. Sandy answered and immediately scolded Christy for not calling her sooner. She had been worrying all this time and was desperate to know how her mother and little sister were doing. Sandy wanted to know everything, but Christy was reluctant to tell her the doctor's prognosis.

Sandy continued to push about Christy's medical condition. She wanted to know where she was getting treatment and how long it would be until she came home. She asked her mother if she was going to have surgery to cut off the ugly tumors that were on her forehead or if they would just naturally disappear.

Tears were sliding down Christy's cheeks. She didn't have the heart to tell Sandy she was dying. She ended the phone call with the promise of calling later. Christy hung up and cried hard into her pillow.

She hadn't listened to the doctors when she was first diagnosed with cancer. She didn't want to believe that the disease was really that bad, and especially she didn't want to believe that her lifestyle might have contributed to it. Now, she thought, the cancer is in charge and I'm going to lose my girls and die.

She was crying when Patti and Natalie walked in. At first she didn't know they were there but then she heard Natalie start to cry. Looking up, she saw Patti, her compassion obvious. Patti knew the news wasn't good.

Patti said brightly, "When we were coming into the room the nurse said you could go home today!"

Giving Christy a big smile she said, "How would you like to come home with Natalie and me for a while?"

Natalie interrupted, "Yes! And then we can read you *Ferdinand the Bull!*" and she looked at Patti for approval.

Patti said, "Absolutely! And I'll bet your mommy would like to see you swing on that tire in the back yard, too!"

Natalie responded excitedly, "Yes, Mommy, let's go now!"

Just then the nurse arrived, carrying the discharge papers. After going over her pain medication the nurse reminded her again that the doctor would like to refer her to hospice but Christy didn't hear her. She kept her eyes on her young daughter, watching her every move.

Christy and Natalie left the hospital with Patti. They drove to Patti's house, Christy silent, Natalie chattering away about toys and books, happy her mother was with her.

When they arrived, Natalie ran to the swing Ron had made for her in the back yard. Now that her mother was with her she was deliriously happy. She told her mother about all the fun she had, the food Patti had fixed for her and the new toys they had given her.

Christy spent the rest of the day watching Natalie play, thinking about her daughter's future, devastated at the thought of leaving her. Patti gave Christy her space, staying in the background, responding when needed.

At dinner Christy tried to eat, but had trouble swallowing. Patti had made mashed potatoes but she could only manage a few bites.

Afterwards Patti helped Christy get her daughter ready for bed. They read the story of *Ferdinand the Bull* and Natalie giggled with delight at a bull smelling flowers.

"That's so funny, Mommy! Have you ever seen a bull that liked flowers?" she laughed. Christy smiled at her daughter and loved her more than life.

Once Natalie was asleep Christy was ready to talk.

"Patti, the doctors told me there isn't any treatment for my cancer. All they can do is keep me comfortable."

Tears were running down her face. She squeezed out the words she was dreading. "I have to find someone to adopt my Natalie." Hiding her face, Christy sobbed uncontrollably.

Patti asked if she had other family who might be willing to adopt Natalie. Christy said there was her mother, but didn't know where she was. They hadn't gotten along for years. She wasn't even sure if she was still alive.

Then she remembered almost two years ago when she was going through a rough time, Natalie had been in foster care. She said the foster parents had been very loving and told her they would always be there for Natalie.

Breaking down, she said Natalie had really liked them and missed the couple terribly when she left their home. She hadn't kept in touch with them but maybe she still had their phone number.

Rummaging through her purse Christy found her address book with their phone number. Even though Patti advised her to sleep on it overnight and make the decision in the morning, Christy couldn't wait. She wanted to call them now, even if it was late at night. She needed to know now.

Both foster parents answered the phone at the same time. Lynn and Tim listened intently while Christy poured out her heart to them. They asked Christy if they could take some time to talk to each other about adopting Natalie and Christy agreed.

She hung up the phone in a trance. Having to find a new family to raise her daughter shook her to the core. The sweet little child sleeping in the next room deserved a mother and a father and so much love that she would never want for anything.

Patti cautioned her to take more time to make the decision but Christy felt pressure to get it done as soon as possible.

As the two women were saying goodnight the phone rang. It was Lynn. She said, "Tim and I have talked and absolutely we want to adopt Natalie. How soon would you want this to happen?"

Christy heard a voice coming from her mouth, "As soon as possible."

"We'll be there tomorrow then," replied Lynn, excited. "We've looked on the map and it should take about 14 hours if we drive straight through!" She added, "Do you know an attorney in town?" Christy didn't but she was sure Patti or Ron did.

She hung up from their conversation with a sinking feeling in her stomach. It was really happening. Natalie would have a new family.

She went into the bedroom and sat beside her sleeping daughter. She stroked her face and hair and leaned over, kissing her gently. Natalie whispered in her sleep and turned over. Christy climbed into bed and laid beside her, staring at her little face, hoping she would remember how much her mother loved her.

Christy woke up the next morning with Natalie kissing her face.

Her daughter was thrilled to find her mommy in bed with her and said, "Mommy, you are the prettiest mommy in the world, and I love you!" Christy grabbed her and hugged her, sending squeals of delight through the house.

That afternoon Lynn and Tim were knocking on the door. Natalie ran to the door and was surprised and happy to see them. She called them Mommy Lynn and Daddy Tim and was immediately comfortable in their arms. Christy could see it was a good solution for her daughter.

Arrangements were made to see an attorney and by the next afternoon they had all the preliminary paperwork completed and were ready to return home, taking Natalie with them.

Patti again encouraged Christy to take her time but she just couldn't. She said she felt like she was going to explode with grief and needed to get Natalie to a safe and loving home. She slowly packed the few clothes and toys Patti and Ron had so kindly bought, knowing she would never see her daughter again.

When they were outside she held Natalie in her arms and explained that she was going to go stay with Mommy Lynn and Daddy Tim because Mommy was so sick. Natalie protested, and didn't want to go, but in the end promises of swimming in Lynn and Tim's pool and all the fun they would have swayed the four year old.

She climbed into the car and Christy leaned in and hugged her daughter for the last time. A small sob escaped her lips but she covered it up with a quick cough. She kissed Natalie and then stepped away from the car.

Lynn and Tim each hugged Christy and promised they would take good care of her little treasure. With tears streaming down their faces they slowly took their seats and buckled up.

Natalie called through the window, "I love you, Mommy! I'll see you soon! 'Bye, Mommy, come get me when you can! Get better, Mommy, I love you, 'bye!"

As the car drove away Christy called out, "I love you, too, sweetheart, have a good life!"

And then they were gone.

Christy, Patti and Ron stood silent for a long time staring into the dark. The silence was so painful no one could talk.

Christy finally walked back into the house, climbed into Natalie's bed and cried herself to sleep. She knew she had made the right decision but it hurt deep into her bones.

Christy spent much of the next day quietly in bed. She allowed Patti to draw her a hot bath scented with soothing essential oils. She soaked in it until it was too cool to enjoy. When she got out, Patti treated her to warm comfortable blankets and hot soup on the veranda. Patti's loving attention helped ease her aching heart.

The next day Christy had Ron take her to the store where Andrea worked. When she walked in, Andrea looked irritated, but covered it with a smile. Christy asked Andrea to take her back to the cabin to get the rest of her belongings. Andrea protested but finally agreed.

Andrea complained she was out a whole month's rent for that cabin. Hearing this, Christy changed her mind and told her she'd go back there and finish out the month. She was thinking that in one month she might be able to get back on her feet, possibly proving the doctor wrong. She was willing to give it a try. At least this was a place she could call her own.

Several days later hospice received a referral from the doctor who had treated Christy at the hospital. The address said only, 'cabin along the river, 30 mile marker.'

The second referral came shortly afterwards from Patti, who had called, worried about Christy. It had been five days since Andrea had picked her up and there had been no word. She was sure Christy would need help, alone in the cabin.

Armed with this information we drove down a two-lane highway along the river, looking for a dirt road near mile marker 30. The road was easy to find and we turned at the dirt road towards the river.

The hospice team was comprised of me, the medical social worker, and Percy, the director of nursing. As we drove up to the cabin a small black bear scampered off towards the river.

We knocked on the door and a young teenage girl answered, looking like she had the weight of the world on her shoulders. She stared at us anxiously.

We introduced ourselves and told her the doctor had sent us to check on Christy. She looked grateful and said her name was Sandy and she had gotten really worried when she couldn't reach her mother. She had hitched a ride from Huntington Beach and Andrea had brought her to the cabin two days ago.

Sandy invited us to see for ourselves how sick her mother was. Christy was lying on her right side in a big four poster bed, covered up except for her face.

Her forehead was darkened by two large tumors the size of golf balls. When we turned on the light Christy groaned and covered her eyes.

She sat up when she realized there were strangers in the cabin. She listened to why we were there. It became obvious by Christy's moans and groans that her pain was severe. We offered nursing visits, pain medicine, and support at no cost to her. But in the end Christy did not want hospice service and sent us on our way.

Once outside I gave the disappointed, tearful Sandy my card and told her where the nearest telephone was, and suggested that she call hospice if her mother changed her mind. I encouraged her to call 911 if she feared for her mother's life.

We drove away from the cabin with Sandy standing on the porch, looking forlorn and miserable.

The next day Sandy called and asked us to come back and talk to her mother again.

She blurted out, "I'm afraid my mother is going to die in that stupid cabin! I tried to get her to let me call the ambulance but she refused. She did agree to let you come back and talk some more, though." I told Sandy we would be there as soon as we could.

This time when we arrived at the cabin, Christy was sitting on the porch in the sun. An attempt had been made to brush her hair and she was fully dressed. She eyed Percy and me with suspicion. Sandy was standing beside her, looking worn and exhausted.

Christy said, "Sandy says you ladies would really like to help me out with my pain and some kind of support. How do you intend to do that when I don't have any insurance or money?"

I told Christy that hospice is designed to support each patient with as much or as little care as they would like. I explained that nurses who work in hospice become the eyes and ears for the doctor and their goal is to provide comfort care. I also added that my job as a social worker was not only to support her and her family emotionally, but to identify any resources that are available to her. Not having money or insurance did not disqualify her from hospice.

Christy admitted, "I can be really nasty when I'm in pain, just ask Sandy," and she looked admiringly at her daughter. "I do need some help, though, and my pain is awful most of the time. At night it's nearly unbearable."

Sandy said, almost embarrassed for her mother, "If it wasn't for the marijuana Andrea left, I think my mom would have gone crazy last night."

She looked tearfully at her mother and said, "You were like a crazy woman last night, screaming at me to clean up the house, or to go get you ice cream, or for me to stop the pain. You were crazy and scary. Once I got you to smoke that joint you were more yourself, but still a little crazy." Sandy put her hand on her mother's shoulder but Christy winced and pulled back.

Sandy said, "See, Mom, we do need these ladies' help. Even with the pot, you hurt."

Christy asked if she could still smoke pot. Percy replied, "What you do with your life is up to you. We don't supply it but we would like to know what you are doing so that we can support you. You are free to do anything you want to do." ·

After Christy agreed to hospice support we left with a long list of things she needed. Pain medication and symptom management were on the top of Percy's list. Financial and emotional support was on the top of mine. I was very concerned about Sandy's welfare.

Pam was assigned to be Christy's nurse. She drove out to the cabin that afternoon with pain medication the doctor had approved and a hot meal the hospice house staff had put together.

Christy was going to need a lot of support. There was no way her young daughter could manage it all by herself.

Even though Christy said she wanted only a small amount of support, her daughter called every day asking for help. Sandy was overwhelmed by the seriousness of her mother's condition, plus caring for her in a remote cabin, which terrified her.

I went to the cabin the next day and talked to both of them about alternative living arrangements. Sandy was all for it. She was tired of sitting in a dark cabin all day and night, afraid to make any noise that would wake her mother up. She couldn't even take a hot shower. Moving to town would ease her worries.

Her mother, however, wanted to stay in the cabin as long as possible. Begrudgingly, Sandy decided to honor her mother's decision, so the two stayed where they were.

Good news came at the end of the week. I had contacted the local Social Security office and requested a TERI Social Security Disability application. Even though the rules are very strict for qualifying for Social Security disability, if a person is determined terminal, the application can be approved within a few days. Christy's disability check would provide her with some income and possibly encourage her to move to town.

With the medical help hospice provided Christy started to feel better. She and Sandy were able to get out of the cabin and walk along the river. They saw a few black bears fishing in the river but none appeared interested in them. They were able to share some tender times, just the two of them, mother and daughter.

When I would come to visit, Sandy would talk about the little things Christy was able to do, like dressing herself without help. And Christy would brag about what a great daughter she had. The two didn't seem to notice that their roles had reversed.

When the disability check arrived, Christy decided to pay the rent on the cabin for another month. Sandy was disappointed but saw that her mother was really happy out in the wilderness. She realized it was her mother's time now and was just grateful to be there with her.

It was very difficult for us to keep in touch with Christy, because she didn't have a phone, so we made arrangements to get her a cell phone.

Even then she didn't always answer it. It became normal for me to visit without letting her know I was coming.

I drove up one day and Sandy was standing outside, clothes flying out the front door as fast as Christy could throw them. By the time I stopped the car I could hear Christy yelling profanities and threats at Sandy. I asked Sandy if she was OK.

She was crying and said, "I really don't know what set her off! We went for a short walk and when she walked into the cabin she started yelling about the mess!"

Sandy agonized, "For the last few days she hasn't seemed like herself! She's been talking about dying and wants me to make arrangements to go back to Megan's house. She wants me to get on with my life. Mom doesn't want me to see her die. She's tired of being sick and she wants to move up to that hospice house you've been talking about."

I knocked on the cabin door and asked if I could come in. Christy said "yes", sending more profanities my way.

She was sitting on the big bed in the middle of the room. I shut the door, leaving Sandy outside so we could have some privacy and asked, "What's going on?"

"I can't do it anymore!" Christy cried. "I can't stand this little cabin! It's cold all the time! I don't want to let my daughter see me die like this! She's been sweet and strong for me, but she deserves more. I want to move to the hospice house and send Sandy home to Megan's parents. Can you help me?" pleaded Christy.

"How soon do you want to move?" I responded. "Of course I'll have to get the doctor's approval but that is just a technicality. What would you like me to do?"

"Just make sure Sandy is able to go home," Christy said, gratefully. "It's horrible to have her see me look this way."

Christy showed me a new tumor that was starting on her neck. It looked red and painful. I told her I would make the necessary arrangements to get her into the hospice house but how did she plan on getting Sandy back to Huntington Beach? Christy said she would ask Andrea for a favor and see if she had any friends going that way.

For the next week Christy promised every day to move into the hospice house and let her daughter help her decorate her room. But each day she came up with a different excuse why she couldn't.

Delays like this are not uncommon. In Christy's case the move meant she would have to say a final goodbye to her oldest daughter and acknowledge that she really was dying. She was not ready to do either one.

Hospice continued to medically and emotionally support her while she lived at the cabin. Whenever she wanted it, her room would be waiting for her.

Meanwhile, the thought of Christy's young daughter riding back with a total stranger for 14 hours really bothered me. I decided to see if I could raise enough money to buy her a plane ticket home.

The hospice staff pitched in what they could and I contacted a local woman's organization who added enough money so I was able to purchase the ticket.

When I shared the good news with Christy and Sandy that she could now fly home, they were both relieved, but still not committed to when it would happen. Sandy asked me to contact Megan's parents to see if they would take her back. She had left without telling them and hadn't been in contact since.

I spoke with Judy, Megan's mother, and explained the situation. She said they would welcome her with open arms. She, too, had lost her mother as a teenager and understood the turmoil Sandy was going through. She assured me they would also find a good counselor for Sandy, to help her with her grief.

Monday morning I received a call from Christy. She asked if the offer to fly Sandy home was still valid. I said it was, and asked how soon she wanted to leave. She said as soon as possible, so I scheduled the trip for the next day.

When I arrived with the ticket Sandy was going through her mother's meager belongings. Christy wanted her to have some mementos even though there wasn't much to pick from.

The next day I checked to make sure they were ready to go. Christy pleaded and asked if Sandy could go another day. I told her no, the ticket was only valid for that flight and it was scheduled to take off in just a few hours.

Andrea was contacted and reluctantly drove Christy and Sandy to the airport with just minutes to spare. The airport personnel whisked Sandy through the doors and then she was gone.

It had happened so fast Christy had forgotten to get a final hug.

Christy called me at the hospice house, wailing into the phone, "I forgot to give Sandy a hug goodbye but I can't go back, I'm halfway to the hospice house and Andrea says she won't turn around anyway. Please help me, Joanne!"

I tried to soothe what I thought was a sad and grieving mother. But she responded with, "I'll probably still have to go back." Curious, I asked why she would have to go back since Sandy's flight had already left.

"I don't know," Christy answered offhandedly. "This cop called me and said he wanted to talk to me. I'm in too much pain. Can you take care of it?"

I said I would. I called the number and a gruff voice answered. The police officer informed me that Sandy had been arrested just before she got on the plane. She had over an ounce of marijuana and drug paraphernalia in her possession.

"The problem is," he said, "someone will have to take temporary guardianship of her, because her court appearance won't be scheduled for at least another fifteen to twenty days."

I explained that Sandy's mother was dying and there was no other family available. I also explained that the drugs and paraphernalia were probably her mother's, and it was probably coveted as a keepsake.

While it hadn't been good judgment on Sandy's part, she obviously didn't realize her bags would be searched before she boarded the plane.

I told the officer my concern was to get Sandy on the plane and back to her foster parents.

The police were stymied. Later that afternoon a youth authority judge called and asked me what WE were going to do about the situation.

"Nothing," I replied. "I don't have Sandy, you do. If it was me, I'd drop the charges and let her get back to her guardians and get into the counseling her foster mother has set up for her."

That night, at 11:30 p.m. Sandy, escorted by a police officer, got off the plane at Huntington Beach and fell into her foster mother's arms. Judy   gathered up the sobbing teenager and took her home.

The next day Christy moved into the hospice house.

Her first day there she felt miserable. She tearfully told me that since she had lost both her daughters she no longer had the will to live.

Her pain became difficult to control. I helped her through her anxiety, guilt and grief using Meridian Tapping Techniques (page 216). I reminded her that she had taken the loving responsibility to   secure good homes for both her children. In her condition that was all she could hope to do.

Her second day was much better. She received her medication on time and in the proper doses. Patti and Ron visited her and she felt good enough to go for a ride with them.

"Today," she announced, "is the first day of the rest of my life!"

Christy liked being treated like a queen. She realized that she could ask for just about anything and it would be done. She surprised me by asking to find her mother, wherever she was, and to tell her that she was dying.

"What is her name and do you have any idea where she is living?" I asked.

She told me her name was Ruthie Nelson, but she had remarried and wasn't sure if her name had changed. She said her stage name had been Kitty Kit Kat. Overcome with emotion and tears rolling down her cheeks, she said, "It's ridiculous but I think I'd like to tell her that I forgive her and love her, before I die." I assured her I would do the best I could to find her.

Based on the information Christy gave me I found her mother after the ninth phone call. I explained Christy's situation and asked if she would be willing to speak to Christy.

"Hell yes, I want to talk to my baby!" she boomed.

I connected her to Christy's room and the two cried more than they talked.

The following day an old RV pulled into the parking lot of the hospice house. On the sides were printed in large gold letters, *Kitty Kit Kat Dancer Extraordinaire.*

The door opened and out stepped a heavyset woman poured into tight blue jeans. Her bright pink cowboy boots matched her bright pink billowing blouse and she was carrying a purse that was a miniature version of a western saddle.

She walked in and announced in a haze of perfume that she was here to see her daughter Christy.

A timid little man followed and stood quietly beside her. I asked them to step into my office for a few minutes while I explained Christy's condition to them.

As soon as Ruthie settled in her chair and put her saddle purse in her lap she leaned over and said in a heavy Texan drawl, "I ain't one for idle chit chat, you said my baby is dying. Why the hell are we parked here instead of right beside my sweet angel's bed?"

Her husband John said in the same Texas drawl, "Now, darlin', we jes' got here. Let the lady have her say." Ruthie bristled and told him to shush. John sat back in the chair and shook his head at his wife.

"OK," Ruthie demanded, "tell me what you've got to say about Christy so we can git to seein' her."

I explained, "As I told you on the phone, Christy is dying from cancer. What I didn't tell you was that her cancer is very visible. It appears as lumps on her body. The ones on her face bother her the most. When you first see her it could be a shock. Telling you about them now will hopefully prepare you and spare Christy any embarrassment."

"OK, I can deal with some lumps and bumps," Ruthie said impatiently. "When do you think she is going to die?" She looked over at John and said, "'cause I have a gig coming up and we can't stay too long."

"Well," I said, "the doctor does not think she has a lot of time left. She isn't eating much but she is still drinking some liquids. We just don't have a crystal ball to know exactly when, but as she gets closer to death the hospice staff will let you know."

Ruthie pursed her lips and said, "Where are Christy's kids, anyway?"

"They went to new families in Huntington Beach," I replied.

"Good, 'cause I'm a professional dancer and don't have time for any kids yippin' at my feet!"

John whined, "Ruthie," and shifted uncomfortably in his seat.

"Ruthie nuthin'! I have my career to think about!" she snapped.

I asked if she had any other questions I could answer. Ruthie got up as fast as her bulk would let her and said, perfume billowing everywhere, "Yes, where's Christy's room?"

I walked the couple down the hall of the hospice house to Christy's room and Ruthie rushed in, saddle purse flying onto the bed.

"Oh my God!" she yelled. "What has happened to my baby? You look worse than something the cat drug in, and those lumps on your face are ghastly! Have you looked at yourself in the mirror lately? Good God! They tried to warn me how bad you look, but they didn't use enough ugly words to get the point across!"

I was right behind Ruthie. Christy looked at me with tears in her eyes. She shook her head and looked at her mother and said, "Mama, I'm dying and I don't care what I look like." But I could tell the words her mother spoke cut deep.

"Mama, it was kind of you to drive all this way to see me. I wanted a chance to tell you I think I understand why you left me all those places and with all those people when I was growing up."

Christy had Ruthie's full attention. "I think you were just overwhelmed with trying to make a living as a dancer and you didn't know how to be a mama. Your mama did the same thing to you."

Ruthie, now bawling loudly, was sitting beside Christy. John patted her on the back and tried to soothe his wife but she pushed him away.

"I tried to be a good mama, but you didn't appreciate the fact that I was born to be a dancer. You were always wantin' or needin' something, so I had to leave you, but it wasn't because I didn't love you, I did, I mean I do. We just had different priorities."

Christy held her mother's hand against her cheek. "Mama, I want to tell you that I love you, and when I die I want you to remember this very important fact. I can't say I ever really understood you," she laughed slightly, "but I do love you."

Ruthie replied, "Well I love you, too, baby." She stood up, grabbed her saddle purse off the bed and opened it up.

She pulled out $200 and gave it to Christy, saying, "This is for something special." Christy sat there stunned, her mouth open in disbelief.

Ruthie turned and headed for the door. John got up and sheepishly fished in his pocket and handed Christy another $200.

"We love you, baby," Ruthie called as she walked out the door. "Maybe we'll stop and see you next time we're through this here little town." John threw a goodbye kiss and a wink, and ran out after his wife.

Christy called softly, "Have a good life, Mama, you take care, John."

And they were gone.

I followed the couple outside, a little shocked at their quick departure. Ruthie turned, faced me and with a bit of a snarl said, "Why didn't you tell me she looked that way?"

"I tried to prepare you, Ruthie," I replied.

"Well you didn't try hard enough!" she stormed. "Haven't you people ever heard of makeup? She would look a lot better with a little foundation and blush!" With that she turned and said, "John, get in!"

In a mixture of exhaust and perfume I watched as they drove away. Ruthie waved a red checkered hankerchief out the passenger side window, and then they disappeared.

I walked back to Christy's room, bracing for the worst and was surprised to find a very happy patient.

Christy exclaimed, "Wow, now I can send $200 to each of the girls! It's not a lot but it's something so they know I care."

After Ruthie and John came for their visit, Christy didn't have any more special requests. She seemed content with her fate and enjoyed talking about her life and what she thought her children would be when they grew up.

Patti and Ron started visiting regularly. Occasionally when Christy felt up to it they would take her for a ride. They were strangers who had become family.

Christy was grateful for their companionship. Patti shared with Christy that she had given birth to a daughter, Tara, 37 years ago, coincidentally on the same day Christy was born. Her daughter had only lived a few hours.

Patti had always wondered what Tara would have been like. Today she was caring for Christy as if she was her own daughter.

Christy's decline became more rapid. The cancer was using more calories than she could consume and her weight plummeted. In just a few weeks she lost 40 pounds and the tumors clearly protruded from her face, head and body. Her complexion changed to a dark yellow green. Pain was her biggest challenge and the hospice nurses tried to balance her comfort medication with her preference to stay alert as long as possible.

A week before Thanksgiving Christy announced that she would live at least until then. She planned what she would eat with Patti, even though she could no longer swallow.

Patti brought recipe books in and when Christy could concentrate they would talk about special dishes they would prepare.

During that week she was in and out of consciousness. Patti would sit beside her and stroke her hair, hold her hand or just read to her. Christy seemed soothed by her voice.

The night before Thanksgiving Christy woke and was tearful and sad. She whispered, "Patti, I look so hideous! How can you stand to be here with me?"

Patti leaned over her bed, stroked her hair and said, "Child, you are not hideous, you are the most beautiful girl I have ever known, and when I look at you I see your amazing heart."

"This isn't how I wanted my life to end, Patti! Christy cried. "I could have been so much better! I could have been the woman you see in me!"

Patti soothed her,"Oh, phooey, better isn't a way to measure your life, you did the best you could under the circumstances, kiddo. I think you are a very brave, remarkable young woman. You are perfect just as you are."

Christy lay there for a long time, either resting from the exertion of talking or just thinking about what Patti had said. She readjusted herself and looked right at Patti. "Do you think we are here on earth to learn lessons?"

"Yes, I do believe we are learning life lessons all the time, Christy," said Patti.

Christy smiled faintly and said, "Then if that is so, I have learned what it feels like to be unconditionally loved by a mother." Her eyes brimming with tears she said, "I love you, Patti."

Christy didn't wake up for Thanksgiving. She lapsed into a coma. It lasted three long days and nights. The hospice nurses kept her clean and out of pain. Patti didn't leave her side. Ron brought her food and shared the vigil with his wife.

Christy died in the wee hours of the morning, Patti holding her hand, encouraging her to go to the light.

In the end she struggled with her last few breaths. When she was gone, Patti sat with her for a while and read her the story she had most requested, *Clifford's Good Deeds* by Norman Bridwell.

Ron and Patti paid for Christy's cremation. She would have qualified for an indigent cremation but Patti wouldn't hear of it. Her remains were scattered in the rose bed in Patti and Ron's backyard.

Epilogue

Natalie has settled into being with her new family. Lynn and Tim felt it was important for her to get some grief counseling so they arranged for her to go to a play therapy psychologist who specializes in childhood loss.

Sandy is living with Megan's family but is having some adjustment problems. She has refused any grief support. Unfortunately, her grades are suffering and she is truant quite a bit. Judy has tried many different ways to support her but Sandy has resisted getting close to anyone since her mother's death.

Judy and Lynn have made a point to get the two girls together. Sandy and Natalie spent Christmas Day together. Tim and Lynn often hire Sandy to babysit Natalie since they live so close.

Ruthie stopped by the hospice house one day and was surprised to discover her daughter had died. She claimed she hadn't been told of the possibility and left angry in another cloud of perfume and exhaust. She didn't inquire about her grandchildren.

Patti and Ron both accessed our bereavement support group and are doing quite well.

Andrea did not visit Christy during her stay at the hospice house and has not accessed any support.

Hospice was there to support Christy and honor her self-determination. Her life was complicated and chaotic but we tried at all times to support her. Because of hospice intervention she was able to make sure her daughters had new families. She also got the opportunity to say I love you and good-bye to her biological mother.

Christy found out what it was like to be accepted exactly as she was. She died feeling unconditional love, thanks to the kindness of strangers.

And in the end, it's not the years in your life that count. It's the life in your years.

ABRAHAM LINCOLN

CHAPTER 6

For The Love of Family

They were high school sweethearts, married for 18 years. Gerry and Penny had met at a homecoming dance at a rival high school. Neither Gerry nor Penny graduated from high school. They were more excited about starting a family and chose to marry instead of continuing their education.

Gerry and Penny were devoted to each other. Still in their thirties, they had worked long hours to save up enough money for a down payment to buy a house. They had lived in this home for the past eight years and were raising two sons.

Penny worked as a maid during the day and as a waitress in the evening. She also had a small business on the side, filling candy machines at the local grocery store.

Gerry owned his own automobile repair shop. It was a small one-man operation and he enjoyed a great reputation with many loyal customers.

Their twin boys, Dan and Ken, were 17 years old. Dan was a gifted athlete and Ken a straight A student. Gerry and Penny had hopes they would each be good enough to get a scholarship. They were good kids and helped Gerry out in the shop and worked odd jobs to make extra money.

Gerry loved dreaming with his sons about what careers they might like. He wanted fewer struggles and more success for his boys. He was sure they were both winners.

It was a fall evening in October when Gerry started experiencing pain and uncontrolled vomiting. Early the next morning he finally allowed Penny to take him to the emergency room because he could no longer stand up. He was diagnosed with an inflamed gallbladder and had emergency surgery to remove it.

Penny and Gerry had always struggled to pay the bills, so a decision had been made to have a high deductible on their insurance to keep their monthly premium down. It was a gamble they had to take, and with Gerry's surgery Penny was grateful they had it.

She pulled the money out of their meager savings to pay the $5,000 deductible, confident their insurance would take care of whatever else came up.

The problem was Gerry didn't get better as expected. He started getting weaker and continued to have nausea and stomach pain. He went back to the doctor, but was told it would just take time to recover.

Gerry went back to work because, he said, "If I can't work, we can't pay the bills."

He worked slower but the boys helped out. Penny noticed that Gerry was starting to look a little yellow so they went back to the doctor. Gerry collapsed at the doctor's office and was admitted to the hospital for more tests and observation.

Penny said there were tests and more tests, biopsies and CT scans. A second specialist was assigned to his case, then a third.

Penny said she lost track of who was who. She said Gerry's hospital room became a revolving door of medical personnel. In the end, Gerry was diagnosed with pancreatic cancer that had metastasized to his liver. Chemotherapy, the oncologists said, was the only treatment that could stop his cancer. Gerry asked about the costs. But no one could tell him and he was too weak to really press for an answer.

Penny assured him they had insurance. She saw this as a fight for her husband's life and wasn't worried about the cost.

The hospital bills started to arrive and Penny kept them organized because she knew her insurance would eventually pay them. Gerry was worried about how this new diagnosis and the medical costs would impact his family.

Penny eventually started hiding the bills from her husband. She knew Gerry would refuse treatment if it put his family in financial ruin.

Penny had been told that since this was a new diagnosis the insurance company would require another $5,000 deductible. Penny didn't have enough savings to cover it so she borrowed the money from her mother. Penny promised to pay her when they got back on their feet.

Days became weeks, weeks became months and Gerry wasn't getting any better. He had round after round of chemotherapy which seemed to make him sicker. The insurance company was paying most of the bills less 20 percent, which was their co-pay, but the bills just kept piling up.

Penny lost her job at the hotel because of all the days she missed. She kept working as a waitress at night because the boys could help out after school. Gerry was so sick he couldn't be left alone. Dan and Ken tried to keep the auto repair shop going on the weekends but they were not the skilled mechanics their dad was. Penny's mother helped financially when she could, but it still wasn't enough. The family was rapidly losing ground.

In late March Penny opened a letter from their insurance company notifying them that Gerry's insurance had been canceled. It explained that he was covered up to $350,000 for a single illness and Gerry's treatment had gone beyond that cost. Penny frantically called the insurance company, trying to understand exactly what the notice meant.

An operator informed her that Gerry's medical needs were no longer the insurance company's problem. Penny said the operator told her they could continue paying premiums for the rest of the family but coverage for Gerry's cancer was no longer an option.

Penny said, "I just stood there, holding the phone, staring out the window. I couldn't believe what this voice over the phone was telling me."

Penny knew that just the hospital bills for Gerry's multiple stays and chemo treatments were over $550,000. She was getting medical bills daily.

She continued to hide the bills from Gerry. Penny knew he was already worried about making the house payment. She didn't want him to know about the medical bills, too. She covered the best she could and focused on helping Gerry.

Gerry's toughest challenge was his abdominal pain. The pain would start coursing through him like electrical explosions, each becoming stronger than the next. He feared every pain attack. At first he had to contend with them two or three times a day, but after a month the attacks happened twenty times or more daily.

As the pain became more profound he also developed a dull, aching pain under his right arm that was always present, pressing down on him every waking moment. He tried all kinds of pain medication. Some worked for a short time but eventually almost nothing worked. As the doctor prescribed stronger pain medication, the cost increased, too.

Penny started selling everything they had that was worth anything. Because of her desperation most of her treasures went for pennies on the dollar. She had garage sales and even sold furniture from the house. She borrowed money from all her relatives but it was never enough.

In May, Gerry was rushed to the hospital with uncontrolled pain. While he was in the emergency room the insurance problem was identified and the hospital social worker helped Penny apply for Medi- Cal (a medical insurance program for low income families in California, page 128).

Penny was not aware of Medi-Cal as an insurance option. The social worker told her the family would have to qualify financially, but with the small income from her waitress job and no savings she believed there would be no problem.

Gerry came home from the hospital even weaker, unable to keep anything down.

Penny said, "He was disappearing before my eyes."

It usually takes about 45 days for Medi-Cal to be approved. Penny received an answer after just three weeks. When she opened the envelope she could see the words DENIED stamped firmly on the application before she even unfolded the letter.

She sat down and slowly read the letter. They were allowed to have one car for transportation, but DMV records showed they had fifteen cars registered. She called the Medi-Cal office, confident there had been some kind of mistake, but it was not so.

Gerry had 14 cars that were non-operational registered under his name.

Penny asked Gerry why he had so many cars, cars she was not even aware of. Gerry sheepishly explained that when one of his customers couldn't pay the bill but had a car they could trade for the money owed, he would take the car as payment.

Gerry's plan was to fix the cars later and sell them for a profit. He said they were his savings account for a rainy day, possibly for the kids' education and maybe for the honeymoon they never had.

Some of the cars, he said with a grin, were going to be just for supplying parts he needed to rebuild his old '57 Chevy.

None of the 14 cars were actually running at the time but Gerry did have reasonable plans for them. The cars were stored at a tow truck business owned by one of his buddies. Penny noticed that Gerry's eyes brightened up when he talked about those cars.

Penny called the Medi-Cal worker identified on the paperwork and explained the situation. She thought surely they would understand the circumstances.

The Medi-Cal worker explained the cars were considered assets and would have to be sold at blue book price. The Medi-Cal worker was very sympathetic but was unable to change the outcome. She told Penny that until the cars were sold and a DMV search revealed they no longer owned them, Gerry would not qualify for Medi-Cal.

Penny felt the world lying heavy on her shoulders. The problem was she couldn't sell the cars for blue book value unless they were operational. And Gerry was too sick to fix them.

Understanding the financial spot his "rainy day car fund" had gotten them into, Gerry had Penny drive him to his shop to work on the cars. He stood for about 10 minutes before he had to sit down and rest. Penny handed him the tools he needed and together they tried to get the cars repaired.

The enormous effort took its toll on Gerry and his pain became difficult to manage. They decided to try to fix the cars another time. Penny got Gerry back into the family car and started home.

Penny had given Gerry his last pain pill when he was working on the cars so she stopped at the local pharmacy to refill the prescription. They waited in the car until it was filled.

Gerry insisted on going into the drug store himself. When he slowly walked back out he was empty handed. He got into the car and said, "Let's go." But Penny wouldn't drive away without the pain pills.

Looking at her sick husband she asked him, "How much?"

Gerry just shrugged and said, "Too much."

Penny said, "We can't go home without those pills. I won't watch you suffer if I can help it!" She got out of the car and went into the store.

The pharmacist, George, was waiting for her. He knew Penny from the many times she had picked up medication for Gerry. He had been surprised to see Gerry, as sick as he was, picking up his own medication.

"When the bill was rung up in the cash register Gerry just turned and walked away," George told her.

The pain medication cost $200 for a ten day prescription. George told Penny he could sell her the medication by the day, if that helped.

Penny knew George was being kind, and appreciated his trying to help. But no one understood their financial situation. They wouldn't have any more money tomorrow, or the day after that. They were broke. Penny pulled out her checkbook and wrote a check for $200. She knew it would bounce but would deal with it later.

She walked out of the store holding the valuable medication, shaken to her core.

Big George the pharmacist, as his friends called him, was concerned when he saw the condition Gerry was in. Because of the strength of Gerry's medication and his thin, yellow condition he predicted Gerry did not have long to live.

He called hospice and made a referral. George knew hospice would contact Gerry's doctor and identify if Gerry qualified for hospice care. He also knew that if Gerry's doctor predicted he had less than six months to live hospice would have ways to decrease the man's suffering. George knew they needed help as surely as he knew that Penny's check for the medication would bounce.

Hospice contacted Gerry's doctor and he agreed that Gerry had less than six months to live. He commented that Gerry had missed his last appointment and believed with the rapid progression of the disease that he didn't have long. The doctor requested hospice to visit this man and his family and talk to them about what hospice could offer.

Penny wasn't happy to hear from us but she agreed to listen to a presentation about the hospice program "but only if it won't cost anything."

The hospice team was Casey, a nurse, and me. We were greeted by a very distressed couple. Gerry told us they could not pay one more dollar toward his medical care. Gerry lamented about his illness and his worry about his family.

Casey and I could see Gerry was in terrible pain but was trying his best not to show it. Gerry said he needed to live, he couldn't afford to die. He was aware of the huge medical bills they owed. He said angrily, "because of me!" He was aware they had not paid the mortgage in two months and the third was rapidly approaching.

Gerry said in frustration, "I'm only 37! I have a family to take care of! I just can't die yet!" But Gerry's pain was so bad he was taking deep breaths between sentences trying to control it.

Casey asked Gerry when he had taken his last pain medication and Gerry replied, "I only take them at night because it is just too expensive to take all day long."

She asked, "What would you say your pain level is from one being almost nothing to 10 being unbearable?"

Gerry stoically said, "About a seven, 'cause I can bear it. I can bear anything except putting my family in jeopardy."

To Casey and me, Gerry looked like he wouldn't live through the week. The whites of his eyes were yellow and his complexion was an olive green. He was now so thin his clothes fell from his shoulders.

Because Penny and Gerry had struggled so hard fighting to save his life neither realized how close the end of Gerry's life really was. Casey and I were sitting in their living room, trying to explain what our support could do for them, and we hoped they would accept it.

Penny said she felt like she had been doing a good job taking care of Gerry. She said, "My biggest fear is that Gerry will have pain that I can't help him with." She talked with a worried look, "Gerry fights hard. The pain he deals with every day would kill most men. At night I sit up with him but there just doesn't seem to be medicine strong enough to help. And he won't take extra pills because he knows we don't have the money for more."

A tear escaped from her eye but she brushed it away. With a determined look she said, "We are in this together! I'm 36 and deeply in love with my husband. I'm not ready for him to die!"

Casey and I explained that hospice care would cover Gerry's pain medication, as strong as he needed. Also any medical equipment he might need related to his diagnosis, plus support staff, including a nurse, social worker and volunteer. I explained that if Gerry had insurance it would have paid for our services but since he didn't, hospice would be provided at no charge.

The relief from hearing this made Penny break down and cry. Soon Gerry was crying, too. They had felt so alone and now they had some hope. They realized that as medical professionals we would help them with the medication, the uncontrolled symptoms and the emotional support they desperately needed.

Gerry sobbed openly, allowing his fear, frustration and sadness for what had happened to him and his family to finally be released.

Casey educated Gerry and Penny about the pain medication. She said, "At hospice we work with the doctor to try to find a balance of pain control and quality of life. We understand you don't want to have too much or too little. But just the stress of pain can kill you. So that will be my focus today. I will be calling your doctor as soon as I leave and we'll discuss options for you. And before this day is through you will have medication that helps control your pain."

Gerry was still concerned about cost, but he did acknowledge his pain was almost unbearable. He decided to trust that hospice would be the answer for him. They both thanked us for hearing their story and doing something about it.

We left with Gerry and Penny sitting side by side in the only chairs she hadn't put up for sale. They were old green armchairs that Penny said no one would buy, even at a garage sale. With hope back, they felt a renewed energy and love for each other.

The next day Casey told me she had been out to see Gerry. Unfortunately, he was declining more rapidly than expected.

I decided to drive out to see them. When I arrived, Gerry's face told the story. The cancer had won. Gerry's color had turned from olive green to dark yellow green. And when he looked at me he seemed to know his time was very limited.

He said, "I'm surprised to see you today. I thought you were coming next week, must not be good news."

I said, "Well, Casey didn't have good news to tell me about your condition so I thought I'd come on out and visit a while."

Gerry replied, "I'm glad to see you anyway. Penny and I liked your reassuring words yesterday, and even though the nurse doesn't agree, I'm actually feeling better now that my pain isn't so bad."

That statement brought Penny out of the kitchen where she was baking an apple pie, a favorite of Gerry's. Penny said that Casey had mentioned Gerry didn't look good and explained why, "but we think Gerry's better today."

She stopped and looked lovingly at him, "we just won't believe he is getting worse."

Gerry ate the apple pie, swallowing it with great difficulty. He knew it meant a lot to Penny for him to eat it, so he sat propped up in the green chair and "yummed" his way through every bite.

When he was done I encouraged Penny to join us for a talk. She hesitantly walked over to the green chairs and faced both of us. She tearfully said, "This isn't going to make me sad, is it? I'm tired of always being sad."

I said, "We need to talk about what is happening. You and Gerry need to know exactly what is occurring so you can say the things I know you want to say to each other."

Gerry interrupted and said, "Doll, she's right, we do need to talk. We've been fighting this blasted cancer so hard that we haven't stopped to talk about the fact that we are losing. I need to talk about you and the boys' future."

Penny said, "I don't want to talk about losing you now. We just started hospice!" Pointing to me she said, "Joanne said the doctor thinks you have six months or less. We haven't even been signed up for 24 hours!" But she knew deep down the conversation had been long overdue. She sat down on the fireplace hearth in front of us.

In an attempt to put things into perspective I relayed back to them their journey through his illness. During the story they listened intently, adding facts that clarified my version of the account.

Gerry added, "That chemo doctor told us he didn't think I would live past Christmas. I guess we showed him, didn't we?" And he smiled a proud smile at Penny.

Eventually the story of their journey ended with the present. I pointed out that Gerry's color could be a sign his liver was not cleaning his blood anymore. He couldn't lie down without becoming short of breath. He also couldn't stand up without help and then could only stand for a few seconds.

Gerry interrupted, "But today, I am not in pain…well, at least not a lot of pain."

And Penny happily said, "And today you ate my apple pie!" We all cheered his victories, the smell of apple pie still floating in the air.

I talked to Penny and Gerry about hope and ways to keep hope alive. Today they could hope for a wonderful conversation about the future. They could hope to tell each other how they felt about each other. And they could hope that they had many days ahead to love and laugh.

I said, "No one knows how or when an individual will leave this world. All I know is that all of us, one day, are going to die. Gerry, I don't know when you will die but it will probably be very soon if your condition continues to decline. I encourage you to talk today about your hopes and dreams for Penny, Dan, and Ken."

Gerry was intently listening. He looked at his wife and said, "Sweetheart, I know you don't want to talk about this, but Joanne makes a good point. We don't know when either of us is going to die, and I want to put some plans together if something happens to you." A mischievous look appeared in his eye as he spoke. They laughed at the same time.

Penny said, "I can't die before you! Gerry, you don't know how to cook or clean!"

Gerry said, laughing, "Now wait a minute! I swept the kitchen floor last year."

Penny laughingly said, "Yes, you did, because I would have killed you if you hadn't."

Gerry, still laughing, turned to me, "You see, I could have been dead already, killed because of a major screw spill!"

Penny, obviously enjoying the banter, said, "I still don't understand what you were doing with that giant can of screws in my kitchen anyway!"

Gerry sheepishly admitted, "I was sorting them on the kitchen counter. They were a great find, a treasure trove of useable screws. The problem was the sizes were all mixed up. In fact I didn't ever get those screws organized. That's something I could be doing right now!"

He continued gleefully, "It was really all your fault, Penny. You came home early and scared me--actually you MADE me spill them on the floor!"

Penny laughed and said, "I can still smell those greasy things when I sweep the floor!"

They both were enjoying themselves and I excused myself and left the couple to continue their conversation.

The next day the report from the on call nurse was that Gerry was struggling and the hospice nurse had been with him most of the night, helping to control his symptoms.

When I arrived, the nurse was leaving. She told me that Gerry was finally comfortable but didn't expect him to live much longer.

I walked into the house and found Penny sitting by Gerry, holding his hand. Gerry had his head back and his eyes closed, but when he heard my voice he said, "We've decided I'll be dying first."

Penny looked at me and said, "No, we decided we'll let nature take its course. Remember, sweet husband?" Gerry smiled.

Penny told me that even though Gerry had a tough time in the early morning hours with pain and agitation, they had taken time before that and really talked about their love for each other.

Gerry added, "And Penny knows that I love her, and I know that she will be fine. And with a mother like Penny our boys will be fine, too."

He kept his eyes closed but continued to follow the conversation. Penny talked about their spiritual beliefs and where they had agreed to meet on the Other Side. Gerry said, "She knows she'll find me in that junkyard down the street. I love to fix cars, so I've decided to wait for her there. Right, doll?" and he opened one eye and looked at her.

Penny nodded lovingly and said, "I would like a chaplain to come and pray with us. I need that, Gerry, even though we're going to meet in that old junkyard." Almost apologetically she added, "We don't go to a church, though."

I told Penny and the listening Gerry that I could call one to come over immediately. Gerry opened one eye and said, "Could you have him hurry?"

I said, "Absolutely."

I walked over and picked up the phone. The first church did not answer their phone. The second one did. After I explained the situation to the chaplain she said she would be right over.

When I returned from the call I noticed Gerry had slumped down deeper in the chair. Penny noticed too and got up to check on him.

Gerry opened his mouth and tried to say something, but brown liquid was bubbling out of his mouth and his words could not be heard.

Penny leaned in and hugged her husband, whispering and sobbing at the same time, "I love you Gerry, remember to wait for me, we'll be OK, I love you and don't you ever forget it."

Penny held Gerry for a long time after he stopped breathing. She knew he was dead. But this was her time to hold on to him as long as she wanted. Eventually, Penny looked at me. "I want to call the school and have Dan and Ken come home."

I made that call, along with calling Casey, the hospice nurse, so she could return to the house and help clean up Gerry before his boys got home.

Casey arrived first, and then the chaplain who was able to comfort Penny with her prayers. Ken and Dan arrived, tires squealing, with panic in their eyes. They stood in the doorway, young gangly teenagers reflecting their father's features. They were afraid of what they would see but confident they were old enough to handle it.

As Ken walked across the living room floor to where his father was, he said, "Last night my Dad told me how much he loved me and how proud he was of who I am. He told me how important it was for our family to stay together and help each other when times get tough."

He stopped. Looking at his father's lifeless body he said, "He told me he was going to die pretty soon and there was nothing anyone could do about it."

With tears running down his face, Ken sobbed, "If he hadn't talked to me last night I wouldn't have told him how glad I was that he was my Dad." And he sat down in the old green chair close to his father, holding his father's lifeless hand in his.

Dan was quieter but moved into the room to stand beside his mother, putting his arm protectively around her shoulder. Dan whispered, "I love you Dad, I'll see you in the junkyard."

And through their tears they laughed a little. The chaplain led them in prayer, taking her cue from Dan and adding a blessing for the junkyard, too, just for good measure.

Once the family was ready, the hearse was called and took Gerry's body. I stayed for a while, encouraging Gerry's family to recount their last 24 hours with him, while I contacted friends and relatives.

When I left, Penny was supported by her mother and many friends, but especially her two boys, who looked so much like their father.

Epilogue

One week after their father's death Dan and Ken turned 18. Hospice didn't have enough time to establish a relationship with them, so when bereavement services were offered, they declined.

It is very common for older teenagers to refuse any assistance with their grief, though it's very useful if they do. Neither Dan nor Ken finished high school. They both opted to get a job immediately to try to help their mother out of her financial problems.

I worked with Penny by calling all the accounting firms that handled Gerry's medical bills, requesting a hardship reduction. Many of the bills were reduced by accessing their charity funds but it still wasn't enough.

Penny tried valiantly to save the house by working three jobs but didn't have a chance. She was too far behind in her payments. Ten months after Gerry died the house went into foreclosure.

I was able to find an attorney who worked pro bono to advise her what to do with the massive amount of bills. She owed over $500,000 for Gerry's medical bills, and that didn't include the credit cards they had been living on when neither could work. The attorney had no other choice but to recommend filing bankruptcy.

Penny has benefited from hospice bereavement support. She says it helped her cope with her grief.

Not surprisingly, she isn't well herself. She works almost 16 hours a day and the stress from the last year of caring for Gerry has taken its toll. Penny visits the junkyard often, and says it brings her some comfort that Gerry is no longer suffering.

Penny had to move from the home she and Gerry loved so much. When they were removing the stove from the kitchen six screws were found under it. They all had a good laugh about Gerry's money-saving schemes. Penny carries all the screws she found in her pocket.

Penny and her sons have moved into a two bedroom home with her mother. The boys are trying their best to honor their father's wishes to help each other. Penny hopes someday the boys will return to school.

Author's comment:

Many times the option of hospice is overlooked because it sounds like giving up. "I'm too young," "I'm not ready," "If we talk about death, doesn't that mean that I am giving up?" "If I ask for hospice, Dad will give up."

Actually, by contacting hospice you can access a great support team of medical professionals and will find people that fight for quality of life. We are proud to say that many people have graduated from our hospice program and are still alive and living well in our community.

Most people are unaware of hospice care until they are forced into it. Some people fight to the bitter end to deny hospice support, as if by denying it the inevitable will be postponed.

People who resist hospice help are often robbing themselves of a supporting, empowering experience. Hospice can be your biggest advocate, medically, emotionally, financially, and spiritually.

Using hospice services may actually lengthen one's life. Unfortunately, there wasn't enough time left to show Gerry what hospice could do. It was able to give him the opportunity to tell his family how much he cared for them, and he died comfortably.

That in itself is a treasure to Penny, Dan and Ken.

There are only two ways to live your life. One is as though nothing is a miracle. The other is as though everything is a miracle.

ALBERT EINSTEIN

CHAPTER 7

Tapping into the Present--
A Love Story

Max and Sara were a fun loving, middle-aged couple newly retired, with exciting plans to travel the United States in their brand new motor home. Sara was a seven-year breast cancer survivor. She was confident her cancer had been eliminated. She took excellent care of her body, ate the right things and got regular checkups.

Sara was joyfully in charge of planning what they would pack in the RV. Max helped, and with their arms full of food, linens and clothing, they eagerly packed for their adventure.

While climbing up and down the stairs, Sara noticed that her back and ribs were aching. She realized she was getting tired to the point of exhaustion after just a few hours of preparing for their trip. She thought it must be arthritis but didn't want any complications during the trip, so she made an appointment with her doctor.

Sara went alone, sure that her doctor would just write a new prescription and she would be on her way. When the doctor probed deeper about her pain and exhaustion she realized she might have misjudged her symptoms.

The doctor ordered tests. A week went by quickly and the couple finished their trip preparations. When the doctor's office called they requested that Sara and Max make an appointment to discuss the results. Sara really didn't want to know what the doctor had to say. By this time in her heart she already knew the news was not good. But with Max at her side they heard the news together.

The tests were conclusive. Sara had a different type of breast cancer. This time she also had tumors on her ribs and spine. The doctor talked about many different treatments but none, he said, would really increase her life.

To be sure, Sara wanted a second opinion, and went to see the oncologist she had used for her first cancer seven years ago. The oncologist didn't sugarcoat it--Sara's prognosis was poor.

Sara faced a tough decision. Did she want to receive chemotherapy? It might increase her longevity but could possibly reduce the quality of her life. The oncologist could not guarantee a positive outcome even if she did complete all the treatments.

Max and Sara decided to wait to answer the question.

The oncologist encouraged Sara to make up her mind quickly. Sara had learned from her last bout with cancer that what he was asking could impact the rest of her life. Their future was riding on the decision. Sara and Max wanted to talk to the family before giving the oncologist an answer.

Max and Sara called their four adult children to come to their home for a family meeting. The kids and their spouses arrived and were told the news of Sara's cancer and the grim prognosis. The treatment was discussed, the side effects, and the probable foreseeable conclusion, even with treatment.

All of them argued for their mother to be treated at all costs. They wanted their mother to prove the doctor wrong. The kids saw no reason not to fight for her life. They argued that she had many reasons to live and one was to see her grandchildren grow up. Each family member was given an opportunity to be heard.

Then Sara got a chance to speak. Sara didn't want to die, she had a wonderful family and a wonderful future planned, but the cancer had changed her life focus. She wanted to live the rest of her life loving Max and the rest of her family without being sick. She didn't want to give up the time she had left to doctor's appointments, treatments and side effects.

Sara told the family she would choose life on her own terms, without intervention. She asked each of her children to help honor her wishes.

Sara's daughters understood immediately and agreed to do anything they could to help. Her sons protested. They didn't understand how their mother could just decide to let nature take its course. They knew her as a fighter. She had always expected the best from them. Now it was their turn to discuss what they believed would be the best for her.

It was Max who stopped the dispute. He stood up at the end of the dining room table and with tears in his eyes said, "Your mother is doing the best she can. She has always believed in living the best life and sharing that adventure with each of you. Today and into the future your mom and I are asking that you support us to continue to live with that passion and love."

Max took a deep breath, sat down and looked lovingly at Sara. The sons could see the decision had already been made and with heart-wrenching resolve, agreed and offered their love and support.

For a while Max and Sara continued taking short trips away with friends and enjoyed their time together. They watched old movies, took walks and generally lived their life trying to capture every day together.

Eventually Sara's pain became difficult to control. She didn't like to feel drugged so she resisted taking her pain medication. She realized that the life she so bravely talked to her children about was disappearing.

She turned to her family doctor, asking for better drugs. The doctor told her he believed she had less than six months to live. He recommended hospice. He said hospice could help her continue to live life with better quality and it would help resolve some of her pain issues.

Sara and Max again called the family to come to the house. As a family they met the hospice team and learned what was available to Sara and each one of them.

They were encouraged when they discovered that hospice patients usually live with more quality and less pain than those who do not choose hospice. The patient and family are supported by an interdisciplinary team that addresses the issues connected to having a terminal illness. They learned that hospice is a support team designed to enhance their life, not change it. Sara would not have to leave her lovely home. The team could provide the care needed right there. With Max and the family helping out, caregivers would not be an issue.

As the hospice social worker I was impressed with the cohesiveness of this family. They were supportive and each willing to do their part to help. It was a wonderful testament to Sara and Max's parenting. It was only after a month of meeting with Sara and Max did I discover they were a blended family. Their communication was remarkable and the love quite apparent.

Sara met with me every week. She was sweet and open. Sad about leaving Max and her family, she was determined to live whatever life she had left. At one of our weekly meetings she announced her obituary was finally finished. It had been the last chore on her list. She encouraged me to read it.

It was a beautifully simple rendition of her life, no frills, just a simple note from a remarkable woman. I looked up and saw relief and pride that she had personally completed this last task. I also noticed pain showing through her smile. Pain I had not noticed fifteen minutes before.

I remarked that she seemed uncomfortable. She tearfully told me that she was experiencing pain often above a seven.

At hospice we use a pain scale 1-10, one means not an issue, ten means unbearable. She said medication controlled the pain for a while but it returned with a vengeance in an hour or so. Usually pain is addressed by the hospice medical staff. However, since pain often has an emotional dynamic, I asked Sara if I could try a technique I use to resolve many emotional issues called meridian tapping (page 135). She said, "Well, I've got medication if it doesn't work, but I'd like to give it a try."

I asked her when this extreme pain started and without hesitation she said, "Six days ago when Max and I quarreled about something really silly. Since then", she said, "he has been distant and cranky."

I asked her if Max would usually hold onto a misunderstanding and she tearfully said, "No, never, he's usually a sweet happy guy."

I asked her where the pain was located and she said around her chest like a tight steel band. I asked her if she could see any colors on it and she replied, "The band is blue and green with red angry swirls in it."

I asked her to rate the level of tightness from one to ten. She said it was an 8. We started talking and tapping.

Sara was very willing and followed my lead. We started on the point on the hand called the karate chop point and she repeated after me: "Even though Max is distant and cranky and I'm not sure why, I do accept and love myself today. Even though I have this tight blue and green band with red swirls squeezing my chest and the pain is an 8, I do honor and accept myself. Even though for some reason Max is distant and cranky, and I have this tight steel band around my chest, which is an eight tightness, I do profoundly love and accept myself today."

She followed the cadence and continued tapping on her meridian points, though at the underarm point, I tapped on myself and she skipped that spot, because of her pain sensitivity.

We continued:

"This tight blue green with red swirls steel band that wraps around my chest, I choose to let it go. This band that causes me pain around my chest, I choose to release it. Max is distant and cranky, what's up with that? The tight blue green steel band around my chest, I choose to release it. Eight pain I choose to let it go. This pain does not serve me; I choose to let it go. Max is cranky, he's never been cranky before, is he getting enough fiber in his diet? (laughing) What if I chose to release this tight steel band that wraps around my chest, would it be ok for me to do that, could I do that, just with this silly tapping?" She was laughing again.

After one round through all her meridians I could see she was feeling better, so we stopped. She took a deep breath and I asked her what her pain and tightness level was. She said it had dropped down to a five. I asked why it was a five and she said she believed that since she has cancer she has to have some pain.

We started tapping again: "This five pain that wraps around my chest, tight blue green with red swirls, feeling like a steel band. What if I let it go, this five pain, could I let it go? Would it be OK to let it go? The cancer has metastasized. Doesn't that mean I have to have pain? What if I could loosen this steel band? What if this steel band pain actually represents hurt feelings and rejection? Could I let it go, knowing that? Just by tapping and looking ridiculous? (Laughter) I choose to let this 5 pain go. I choose to release this pain and tightness into the universe to be used for good." Now Sara was smiling.

She reported that she really couldn't say she was in pain at all and she didn't feel the steel band or see the colors any more. But something still wasn't right. I asked Sara to tell me in a word or two to describe what wasn't right.

She said, "My connection with Max." So we started tapping again, this time more focused on her connection to Max.

"Even though I still feel like I have lost my connection with Max, I do honor and accept myself. I can't put my finger on exactly why I feel this way, it could be I'm afraid of losing Max, or it could be that Max has been cranky and distant which isn't normal for him. Even though for whatever reason I have a shadow left of concern about Max and me, I choose to release whatever it is. Today and every day I choose to focus on living the best life I possibly can in the present tense, and I love that about myself."

We continued tapping through all the meridians, Sara following me. "I am alive and in love with my best friend Max. I am happy that my life is so full of abundance. My friends and family are loving and devoted. Today I have the gift of the present. I honor and appreciate the health I do have. I ask my body to send healing energy throughout my system. I choose to honor my life and make every day the best day possible. Max loves me and I love him. What a great life we have together. I forgive him for forgetting about the present and I forgive myself for forgetting about the present. I choose to make every day count. I am in charge of my focus and I choose to focus on the abundance I do have. I choose to make every day count and I love that about myself."

Sara was truly beaming. She reported no pain and a feeling of overall contentment she had not had since her diagnosis. She asked if I would consider tapping on Max.

I said "Of course I will, if Max agrees." Cancer is a family affair and Max was obviously suffering, too.

I found Max outside in the garden, obviously depressed. He was stooped over, watering some flowers. I asked him what was up. He said that for the past week the realization that he was going to lose his wife "to the blasted cancer" was just too terrible to bear. "I completed my list of things to do, now what do I do?" he said, with sadness in his voice.

He and Sara, with the help of their family, had every detail planned for her funeral. He had sold the RV and their boat and completely cleaned out the garage. He felt like he didn't have anything else to do but sit and wait for the inevitable. He felt worthless to Sara because he couldn't fix her and he felt he didn't have anything to offer her anymore.

He and I talked for a while more and I asked if he would consider allowing me to teach him meridian tapping. He agreed, remarking he would do anything to make the horrible worthless feeling go away. I asked him to rate how worthless he felt, using the same scale I had used with Sara. He said his level was a ten.

We started to tap: "Even though I am completely worthless to Sara and I can't make her better I would like to honor myself today. What's the point? I am losing her before my eyes, I am totally worthless. I feel like I am absolutely useless. Even though there is nothing I can do to make her better, and I feel like an idiot tapping on myself, I would like to profoundly love and accept myself anyway. Even though I feel like I am completely worthless to Sara, I do love her dearly and I love that about myself."

We continued tapping on other meridian points: "I'm completely worthless to Sara. I can't fix it and my To Do list is done. What's the point? There is nothing I can do. I am worthless to Sara now. Well, I'm not completely worthless; I can still mow the lawn. (laughter) And she does get lonely if I'm not around. But I can't fix her cancer and it really makes me mad! (tears) I'm the man! I'm supposed to protect my family and fix things (more tears) and I can't do either anymore! I'm not holding up my side of the bargain, I'm supposed to protect her! (tears) I'm really angry; it's not the way it's supposed to be! We already fought the cancer beast and I thought we won! This is not my dream of retirement! I'm mad as hell and I don't know who to take it out on! I'm worthless, no, I'm not, I'm angry oh, so angry, and I'm frustrated because my To Do list is completely done! But with all this anger and frustration about what I can't do, I'm missing the little things I can do."

I asked Max how his feelings of worthlessness were doing. He blinked his eyes and said, "Well I'll be damned. I think it's not so strong!"

We continued. "What if I let the belief that I have to fix Sara go? What if I let this worthless feeling go? What if I realized that I am wasting time worrying about what I can't change? What if I let this worthless feeling go? It's not serving me and it's not serving Sara. What if I just let it go? Could I let it go? Would I still be a good husband if I let it go? I am a good husband and I love my wife dearly. I would change this situation in a minute if I could but I can't, I am doing the very best that I can under the circumstances."

We stopped. Max seemed a lot lighter. His level of feeling worthless had dropped to a two. And he was smiling. I asked him why he still had a two level left and he said he was a little guilty for wasting time avoiding Sara. We talked more about how useless guilt is. Guilt limits our potential and stops us from living in the present.

We started tapping again, using all the meridian points. "I choose to release any guilt about what I have or have not done in the past. I can't change it and it's a big waste of time. I choose to live my life in the present with love and abundance. I choose to wake up every morning and ask myself how I will make this day fabulous. I am grateful for my wife and honor what a wonderful loving woman she is. I choose to be happy and light and deal with all my life challenges with honor and integrity. I chose to give myself a break when I can't fix it. I am a loving, wonderful husband. My wife loves me, my kids love me, my dog loves me and I love that about myself. I release any useless emotions that keep me from experiencing the present as it should be; full of love and beauty. I choose to see the beauty and abundance that is mine to appreciate every day. I choose to live in the present and appreciate every moment I can with my wonderful wife Sara."

Max looked like he had grown six inches. His posture was straight and he was much brighter. He said he wanted to start with the present right now. He walked into the house and gently hugged Sara and told her how much he loved her. When I left, they were both beaming.

Epilogue

After six weeks Sara's tight steel band had not returned. Yes, she is still a hospice patient, and continues to decline. She still needs pain medication for the physical pain but taps with me to reduce her emotional pain.

She is enjoying each day she has with her kids, grandkids and loving husband Max. When I visit their house now, it is full of music, fresh flowers, light and laughter.

Max takes Sara out often for picnics by the river and on evening drives just to look at the stars. They watch old movies together, holding hands. They report their relationship feels shiny and new.

Max gets up every morning and walks the dog. He tells me, "During the first 30 minutes of the walk I just breathe, then I focus on how I can make my day the best it can possibly be. The last 10 minutes of the walk I think about how I can make Sara's day absolutely magnificent. And I have a very important job. My job is to cherish the moments we have together. I have no control of our future, I just do the best I can each and every day."

Patients and their families are often not able to focus on the present but obsess on the "what ifs," the anger of "why me," and the fear of what is going to happen in the future.

They can also get caught up in all the minutia of chores that have to be done before the end. In short, many rob themselves of appreciating the present and all the abundant gifts that are available.

Meridian tapping helped move Max and Sara into the present. It really doesn't matter how long they will have together. The time they have will be full of quality and love.

None of us has a crystal ball.

All we have is right now, this moment, the present. Anyone living with a terminal illness knows there are lots of challenges ahead, some very difficult. But even in the most trying of times, beauty can be found.

Living in the present is a lesson for us all. No one knows when we or our loved ones will leave this world. Identify what is really important in your life. Try to never sweat the small stuff and always, always, tell family members and friends how much they are loved.

For more information about meridian tapping techniques, go to page 135 or www.eftjoanne.com

Believe, when you are most unhappy, that there is something for you to do in the world. So long as you can sweeten another's pain, life is not in vain.

HELEN KELLER

CHAPTER 8

Finding Honor

Queenie lived in a rough neighborhood. It was one of those neighborhoods where you don't want to stop and ask for directions. Big, beautiful trees lined the street but the front yards sat dry and unloved. There weren't any kids out playing ball or riding their bikes as I searched for the numbers on the houses.

A skinny black dog ducked under a parked car as I drove slowly through the neighborhood, but nothing else moved.

The hospice referral said that Queenie was 72, lived alone and was suffering from liver cancer. As I slowly drove through the neighborhood, I could see in the distance a yard that contained so much garbage it spilled out into the street.

I sent up a little prayer, "Please, not that house." But as I approached the address the numbers got closer and I had a sinking feeling it was my destination. Bailey, the hospice nurse riding with me, said quietly, "Uh-oh."

The house at one point had been painted yellow but most of the paint had peeled off, leaving a dull gray color and sagging windows. I couldn't find a number on the house or the mailbox so I drove past with a sigh of relief. But by the next house I realized it was too good to be true; my destination was the old gray house.

I turned the car around and from the opposite direction I could see that sprawling trash filled the backyard, too, punctuated with broken down cars, four white refrigerators standing side by side, an old rusted out bathtub and a couple of very big dogs chained to the fence. In the middle of the chaos was an old orange van, covered in clear plastic, with the door gaping open.

Bailey and I were the hospice introductory team. I said in disbelief, "I think someone is living in that van!" She was looking in the same direction and cautiously replied, "I sure hope not."

We warily got out of the car and carefully stepped through the front yard trash, plastic bags, broken bottles, old toys and different colored NO Trespassing signs. We walked up to the front of the house and climbed the stairs. The front door was filthy from years of use and neglect. An *"oxygen in use"* sign was nailed to it. But it was the cats huddled around the door that caught my attention.

There were over 20 of them. They were of various colors and sizes but all shared the same tattered look of disease and neglect. My heart went out to them. But our prospective patient would have to agree to hospice care before I could even attempt to do anything for them. I turned and knocked on the door.

It took a while, but the front door eventually opened and there stood a 30 something woman with long, greasy, bright red hair, wearing a tiny string tee shirt and nothing else. She didn't give me a chance to speak. Staring right through me, she slurred, "Mamma's over there."

She pointed in the general direction of the couch and then turned and stumbled off through the house. I couldn't help but notice how filthy she was. Poor hygiene revealed a trail from her backside to the inside of her legs and all the way down to her feet. She walked through the living room and out the back door without saying another word.

We walked into the living room and, from where we stood, we could see through the back window. We watched this almost naked woman climb into the old orange van and shut the door.

A weak voice from the couch said, "Don't mind my daughter. She's just upset about my condition." We both snapped back to why we were there.

Our soon-to-be patient, Queenie, was lying awkwardly on a couch without cushions. The exposed parts of the bare wood frame looked like a giant cat had sharpened its claws on it for the last century. Stuffing had long ago been transformed into millions of cotton ribbons cascading down the grimy, gold-colored upholstery. A pink and white crocheted blanket, which had obviously not been washed for a long time, was covering her.

I looked for a chair so I could sit close to Queenie. I always made it a practice to never sit in upholstered chairs in a house found in this condition. One never knows what's lurking on the cushions.

Just when I had almost given up finding even one chair, Queenie's granddaughter Tina, a thin girl with red hair, came in from school and helped in the search. She brought in a kitchen chair and a piece of wood to replace the chair's missing seat, but the board wasn't big enough. She found another chair after moving a massive amount of clothes and other possessions. Unfortunately, it been used as a cat toilet. Bailey and I decided to stand.

Tina left to join a girl who looked exactly like her, only younger, in the kitchen. We could hear the girls rummaging around in the kitchen apparently looking for an after school snack.

The living room floor was not much different from the yard outside. It was also covered with trash, old clothes, tissues, empty medicine bottles, and soup cans filled to overflowing with cigarette butts. In the corner of the living room stood an old wood stove. Gauging from the chilliness of the room not much wood had been burned. It was throwing a tiny bit of heat but the piles of trash were dangerously close and causing us significant concern.

There was what appeared to be a man sleeping on another well-used couch in the living room. He was covered by a sleeping bag and a dirty blanket. Whoever he was, he was snoring. We squatted down to talk to Queenie about hospice.

She was a little taken aback by the help we were offering her. She told us she was a woman who made her way in this world and didn't want handouts. But when she discovered that hospice would be paid for by Medicare with no co-pay, she agreed to see what we could do for her. Queenie was pleased that she wouldn't have to go to another doctor's appointment. The hospice nurses would be the eyes and ears for the doctor.

As we continued our conversation with her the person on the couch stirred, farted loudly and complained about being disturbed.

No family members sat with Queenie to hear about hospice. It seemed that no one was paying any attention to Queenie at all. This fact, we would discover, had been the status of her life for a very long time.

Hospice always supports self-determination and it's our intention not to change anything unless a patient agrees. But the thought of this woman lying on an old dilapidated couch, silently suffering, was almost too much to take.

Bailey, who was a very experienced nurse, asked Queenie, "Would you like a hospital bed? It would be so much easier for you to get up when you want to."

Queenie looked up from the old couch and said, "I don't know if my son would like that because he doesn't like change. But yes, I think that would be nice, if he agrees."

Her son Al, who was still completely covered up, had apparently been listening to at least some of the conversation. He said, "Yeah, Ma, a hospital bed sounds pretty good. I'm tired of that old stinky thing you're laying on now, anyway."

Bailey ordered the hospital bed and also arranged for a bedside table and a port-a-potty to be delivered that afternoon. Queenie couldn't believe it could be that easy.

We noticed that Queenie was clutching her pain medications and holding them close to her chest. She said her daughter Donna could not be trusted. She said Donna would steal the pain pills if she got a chance. Queenie pointed to her son on the couch and whispered, "He will, too."

She told us that her son wouldn't take the pills himself but would sell them. In the next breath she proudly said he was her favorite child because he always had a job. Al, she informed us, was an alcoholic like his dead daddy, but he did have a job.

She said, "Donna on the other hand is useless. She's a drug addict and turns tricks in the backyard, and she's the no-good mother of my beautiful granddaughters." She sadly told us that Donna could not be counted on to do the right thing, ever.

Queenie's teenage granddaughters were now lying on the floor with the TV turned on, watching cartoons. They seemed to be good company for each other but were oblivious to what was happening to their grandmother.

Concern for this frail woman prompted me to ask if she had eaten recently. Queenie pointed to a plate on the floor with a half-eaten piece of cheese and some crackers on it. She said she wasn't very hungry anymore but if she needed something she could always ask her grandkids to help her. With that statement both girls looked up at their grandmother and grinned.

A good social worker learns to take cues from the environment. Looking into the kitchen I could see the dishes hadn't been washed in a long time. Queenie had probably not had a real meal for quite a while but she might not have wanted one, either.

After Bailey and I finished our evaluations and made our best attempt to tell Queenie that she could call hospice day or night for help, we left. Our wish was to provide immediate support, but we knew that any assistance would have to be with Queenie's permission, and that would probably take a while.

The problems in this household were immense. The teenage granddaughters, Tina and Dee, were minors. From what I could gather, Queenie had been the only responsible adult since Donna had given birth to them. As their grandmother she fought to keep the girls in her home. But after her death they could be facing foster care.

From my interview with Queenie I had not been able to identify any other family members who could be counted on.

It is natural to want to fix a situation. I'm no different than anyone else, but as a hospice social worker my job is to identify what a patient wants at the end of their life and support their wishes. I offer them my respect, then advocate for them to live their life the way they want to, not how I think they should.

Queenie was very sick, living in a filthy home with potential fire hazards, not much food, if any, and very little heat and almost no help. But she was alert and oriented and could make her own decisions. Her hope was to stay and be supported in her home until she died. So that is how I planned on supporting her.

The next day I returned and coincidentally the hospital bed was being delivered at the same time. But, as I found common in this household, some family drama was transpiring.

Al was insisting that the medical equipment delivery man bring a "higher quality" hospital bed, one closer to his mother's standards. Al, it was clear, was very concerned about his mother and wanted her to be comfortable. After some assurances that the bed would be a significant improvement over the couch it was finally allowed into the house.

The old broken-down couch was moved to the granddaughters' bedroom for later use and Al's couch was relocated closer to the hospital bed, where, he said, "I can help Ma when she needs me."

Al was a little over 30 years old and missing all his teeth. He looked a lot like his sister. Although he was unkempt at least he was fully dressed. Through most of my visits he would be passed out on the couch, reeking of cigarettes and alcohol. The blanket and sleeping bag he used were stained with vomit and probably urine.

When he was awake he was threatening. He wanted respect and consideration for the significant contribution he was making, caring for his mother. He often claimed he had been awake all night because his mother had been coughing and vomiting. When I asked Queenie about it she would deny that she had been sick through the night. Queenie was always careful to cover for her son, stating he must have been remembering another time when she had been sick.

Al would often forget that he had used the "awake all night with mom" story. It was obvious that Al wanted the hospice visits to be about him and his contributions. I would spend some time identifying what he was doing because Queenie's care depended on it, and eventually we would get around to her needs.

Queenie needed basic necessities like heat and food. I would ask Al what he was going to do about it. The answer was always the same. "I don't know. I'm too busy to do stuff like that." He would change the subject and want to talk about how much work he did outside the house.

Eventually we both knew he was lying. Al finally told me he didn't have a job, was on probation, and no one would hire him. He had been in jail for long periods of time. Once he reached into his pocket and pulled out some false teeth.

He said, "I got these in jail. Jail is the best place to get new chompers. Doesn't cost a cent and they do a pretty good job, don't they?"

I told Al I had located some donated wood which was available to his family at a local church. I suggested he go pick it up and he agreed. I think he was tired of saying he was a productive part of the family while not having anything to show for it.

Before I left that day Al was in his old pickup truck rattling his way down the road to get some wood. I think his teeth were in his back pocket.

Halfway through my visit Queenie's daughter Donna came into the house from the orange van. She was twitching from coming off some kind of drug, still filthy, but aware enough to know there was a stranger in her mother's house. This time it was a lot colder outside, so she was fully dressed.

Encouraged by Al's response to the wood acquisition, I asked Donna about food in the household. Donna didn't want to have a conversation with me but admitted she had $300 worth of food stamps and was waiting for a ride to take her to town to stock up. I suggested soup for her mother since she couldn't eat solid food. Donna said she would try to remember to get some.

Donnas' twitching was significant and she kept coughing, that deep cough of someone who has been smoking for a very long time. Her upper right arm and elbow were wrapped in a dirty white cloth, the skin red and swollen. It looked like it hurt. I asked if she had seen a doctor and she huffed at me and said, "What for?"

We moved on and I encouraged her to help her mother a little. She said she didn't know what I was talking about.

"I work all day long taking care of my Mama, we're real close," said Donna, indignantly.

I suggested that her mother might like a hot bubble bath and the help to take one. Donna replied, "Mama took a bath last month and that's about all she needs for a while. She's just lying there anyway."

I tried another route, suggesting how nice a warm bath feels for a patient who is in bed all day. Donna didn't hear me. She was busy looking out the back window at a man who was standing beside her orange van, and quickly ran out to greet him.

I knew the hospice nurses would provide a regular bath for Queenie but I was just testing the waters with Donna to see if she was willing to give her mother any TLC. Donna wasn't very responsive and had other things on her mind.

I talked with Queenie, hoping she would tell me how I could help her, but she didn't seem to know how to ask for anything for herself. She didn't complain about her cold house, her personal needs, or her pain. She was physically weak but with some persistence I got her to talk about her life.

Her husband Harold had been a logger and a gold miner. Queenie had often worked like a man right beside him. He had died 10 years earlier from lung cancer. The family lived a hard but adventurous life and she said her children had grown up in the woods. She was proud of her children and bragged about how smart they used to be, but was obviously disappointed that neither had finished high school. She was worried about their future.

She said, "Al and Donna are adults. What I'm most worried about are my granddaughters. What is going to happen to them?"

Together we explored possible relatives or friends who might provide care but none were really appropriate to foster the girls. When we were done, Queenie had a resigned look; she would have to leave their future in someone else's hands. She could do nothing and she knew it.

I talked to Queenie about accessing Medi-Cal as a resource to get In Home Support Services (IHSS) into her home (see Page 128). I explained that with county resources she could hire a caregiver who would help her out for a few hours every day.

Queenie didn't see the need for a stranger to come into her home and help her when she had Al and Donna so close. I explained that Al or Donna could even be paid by the IHSS program for their help but Queenie just didn't want it. She said she didn't like those kinds of programs, and didn't want to add to her problems.

Queenie explained that the house she was living in had been built by her grandfather when he was a young man. The house was the only property she had to pass on to her children. After some discussion it became clear that years of back taxes were owed on the house. Queenie knew in her heart that no one would really inherit the home.

I left the house with more information but still feeling frustrated. Queenie wasn't getting any care, and I couldn't get through to either adult child that she needed help. I was encouraged, though, that Al was picking up wood to warm her home.

Friday nights are a special time for my husband and me. We always pick up a pizza and a movie and head home to relax, the long week behind us. I'd picked out our movie and had driven to the local drive-thru pizza parlor. Coming from the tiny pick-up window I heard, "Hey lady, how ya doin'? Lady from hospice, it's me, Donna!" Through the delivery window I saw Donna waving at me from inside the pizza parlor.

She yelled, "I decided to get my mom some pepperoni pizza! It's on sale so I'm getting two!" and she beamed, smiling a toothless grin, proud she had thought of her mother.

I smiled back and told her how thrilled her mother would be. I had to give her credit--she was thinking of her mother, even though her mother would not be able to eat a bite. It was the thought that counted.

The following Monday, the nursing report stated that Queenie had had uncontrolled pain throughout the weekend and the on call nurse, Abby, had made multiple visits to try to make her more comfortable. Abby said the house was warm and Al was taking an active role in giving Queenie her medications appropriately. She said that Al was in tears and wanted suggestions on how he could help out more. I drove out to their house immediately.

Queenie had noticeably declined. She was very pale, her lips were blue, and she barely acknowledged my entrance into the house. The remarkable thing was that she was clean and the house was warm. The refuse in the living room was picked up and there was soothing music playing from the stereo. Al was trying to encourage his mother to sip some broth but it sat on the bedside table, untouched.

Al looked at me and tearfully said he had really messed up. "She's been sick for a long time, for years, and I didn't really notice. I just thought she would stay this way. I never thought she might die." I reminded him that we had talked a great deal about Queenie's approaching death.

He said, "Heck, I didn't believe you or the nurses. And I sure didn't believe the doctor. I thought, he don't know my Ma, she'll show everybody."

We sat for a long time beside Queenie, and Al talked about life with his mother. I could see Queenie's face while her son talked. Often her mouth curved up with pride when he bragged about how much he respected her.

As Al talked, his demeanor noticeably changed. He sat up straight and wasn't cursing or bragging, just telling it like it was. He was processing his life and his own regrets. He was talking to his mother as a man, no longer as just a son. He knew his mother was dying. He promised her he would do better. He promised her he would take care of her for the rest of her life, and she would feel like a queen. Queenie mouthed, "I love you, son," and fell asleep.

Al sobbed into his hands, clearly feeling the pain of reflecting on his life. He realized he had missed so many chances, and so many opportunities.

After that, Al didn't need any more suggestions about how to make his mother comfortable. With every visit I saw he was more in control of the situation. The kitchen became organized and smelled of homemade soup. The front yard was cleaner and the wood was stacked neatly on the front porch. Al agreed to let SPCA trap the cats on the front porch. He realized they were suffering unnecessarily. He was doing everything he promised his mother he would do, and more.

Queenie rallied during the next few weeks. She really enjoyed being lovingly cared for by her son. She no longer looked at him with disappointment in her eyes, but with admiration. She had released her medication to him; a true test in trustworthiness, and he managed the narcotics with care.

One day when I was visiting, she pointed a finger at him and said, "I always knew he had it in him."

Al smiled when he heard that, and winked at his mother. He was clean, appropriately dressed and wearing his false teeth. His newfound self-respect brought a certain handsomeness to his face.

Al made plans for his nieces, too, and Queenie knew it. Her granddaughters had been helping care for her under Al's watchful eye.

Tina and Dee were eating breakfast, going to school and helping out after school. The TV was no longer blaring in the background. The girls were encouraged to talk quietly with their grandmother, telling her how much they had enjoyed their life with her. They were actually getting a chance to learn who their grandmother was through her stories, and they looked forward, as Queenie did, to their after school visits.

Eventually Queenie lapsed into a coma.

Al listened and learned from the hospice nurses as they taught him how to control her pain and keep her clean. Al sat beside her at night and read out loud from his favorite mechanic magazines. He said she seemed to enjoy his voice. He liked sharing his favorite subject with his mother.

One afternoon Pam, the hospice nurse, and Al had just finished giving Queenie a bed bath. The house was warm and her granddaughters, Tina and Dee, had just finished their homework. All of a sudden from the back yard came barking and people yelling.

It was obvious from hearing the voices that Donna was involved. Al, Pam, Dee and Tina all went to the window to see what the ruckus was about. There stood Donna barely dressed, arguing with a man about some money just outside the orange van.

Al shook his head sadly and turned to Queenie and said, "Mama, some things just never change." His mother was across the room, but something seemed different. Suddenly, he knew she was gone. Pam checked her pulse and confirmed it. His mother had died.

Al sat at the bedside, held Queenie's hand and cried.

Donna was forced to stop her fighting and get dressed. She didn't take the death well. She said she wasn't prepared. Someone should have told her Queenie was dying. She yelled at Pam, trying to make her take back the words of death. She accused Pam of giving her mother too much medication.

Pam had dealt with angry family members before and once again explained what had happened with Queenie. When Donna didn't get any support from her brother or her own daughters she left the house seeking the security of her van.

Al, Dee and Tina sat with Queenie for a while. Al was proud that he had kept his promise and knew he had treated his mother like a queen before she left this world. Even though he was sad he felt satisfaction well up in his chest. He said out loud, "I am the son you knew I could be. Thank you for believing in me, Ma," and kissed his mother on the cheek for the last time.

Dee and Tina softly told their grandmother they loved her. When the family was ready, Pam called the local funeral home and made arrangements for Queenie's body to be picked up.

Queenie died in her grandfather's home just like she wanted to, with the love and support of her son and granddaughters. The hospice team was there for her to reduce her symptoms, increase her quality of life and prepare her for death.

In the end, she was a queen. Al made that happen and was proud of his contribution.

Eight Months Later

Al has been involved with grief counseling and is going to Alcoholics Anonymous twice a week. He is working as an auto mechanic at a local repair shop and attending parenting classes. He is focused on getting his nieces out of foster care by the summer.

Queenie's home was condemned after she died, a tough blow for Al, but he couldn't financially save it. He rented a three bedroom home so the girls could each have a room of their own. Individual bedrooms, Al said, are something they had never had.

Al likes himself now and is always reaching for the man he knows his mother saw in him.

Dee and Tina are in a foster home together. They were very upset about leaving their home to live with strangers, but now admit it's not so bad. Dee said, "The sheets are always clean, and the food is great." But they are really looking forward to living with their Uncle Al.

Neither Dee nor Tina wanted grief support but they did enjoy putting together a large picture album of their life and talking about the impact their grandmother had had on them.

We met once a week for six weeks. We didn't call it grief support; we called it talking about grandma Queenie. They were both very happy to do that. They expressed a lot of grief during those sessions. Queenie had loved them dearly, and they knew it. She will be missed.

Both girls are on the honor roll at school, trying to fulfill their promise to Queenie. Tina said, "Grandma made us swear on our love for her, that we would do our best in school."

She made them both promise that they would go to college, too. They are holding each other to that promise.

Donna was arrested a few days after her mother died, for assault and prostitution. She was arrested in the back yard next to her orange van. She is still in jail.

The two big black dogs in the backyard were taken by animal control and were both subsequently adopted by a young man who thought they deserved a second chance. They are now inside dogs and are very loved, fat and happy.

Those who look for beauty, find it.

UNKNOWN

CHAPTER 9

Jack and the DragonFly

The day the hospice team arrived at Jack's home was a dark day. He didn't want to move and he didn't want a bunch of bossy people telling him what to do. He didn't want to leave his home. He didn't want what he thought hospice represented.

He had lived a life of freedom and wasn't willing to give up any of that just because he was sick. He was scared that he would be forced to leave his home. His sister Anne had talked him into at least finding out about hospice. But he put her off for months, enduring terrible pain and frightening health challenges. He was tough and a bit stubborn. He finally agreed to consider another way of dealing with his pain and uncontrolled symptoms for his sister's sake. He could see the worry on her face. Anne was Jack's older half-sister, sweet and kind, and exhausted from caring for him.

Anne graciously welcomed the hospice nurse and me into her home. The front door opened directly into the laundry room. Across the hall in front of us was Jack.

He was lying on a tiny make-shift bed, black, suspicious eyes and a bulbous nose peering out from under a knitted cap. He was unshaven and his teeth were in a glass by the bed.

The sheets on the mattress were either pulled back or not there, because it was easy to see that the head of his mattress was propped up with a couple of pieces of firewood. The mattress was gray and well used, the blankets old and tattered, but clean.

Jack suffered from chronic obstructive pulmonary disease—COPD—and prostate cancer, which had metastasized to his bones. If he lay flat he became so short of breath he was in danger of suffocating. He was in so much pain from the cancer that had spread to his hips and spine he could hardly sit still. He valiantly tried to mask his discomfort, trying not to show weakness to the strange women standing in front of him.

Jack was a gentleman. He couldn't get up but he offered us a chair. We visited a few minutes and then got down to business.

I explained to Jack that hospice is a medical support team. Our goal is to honor each person as an individual, while attempting to control symptoms and reduce pain. In doing this we would support his sister, too. Jack said suspiciously, "Well, when do I have to go to the old folks home?"

I asked if he wanted to leave his home. Jack said, "NO WAY, I want to stay right here, with my sister!"

I said, "Well, that is exactly what hospice services are designed to do, if that's what you want."

Jack asked, "You mean I have a choice about all this?" I explained that not only did he have a choice he gets to be the boss. We help as much or as little as he wants and he could fire us if he didn't like the assistance. And the best part is it's paid for by Medicare and wouldn't cost him anything.

Jack relaxed and started to smile. He said, "What about my pain? Can you help me with the pain?"

The answer was a big resounding YES. Jack was considering hospice just to help out his sister, but it was becoming obvious that hospice could really help him. He signed the hospice contract.

And thus began Jack's journey with hospice.

Two years previous his sister had invited him to come live with her. He had become so sick he could no longer take care of himself. The untreated prostate cancer and end stage COPD made it impossible to walk even across the dining room floor without stopping to rest.

"Never married, no children, I was a rail rider, a real hobo," he bragged.

He traveled from one end of the country to the other, doing odd jobs when he needed money. He knew to look for good-hearted women who, during that time, would paint an outline of a cat on the back gate, signifying they would feed travelers like him. Freedom is what he sought and most of the time freedom is what he found.

He was an educated man. He displayed his college degree in biology in his tiny room, and his sister bragged he also had a Doctorate in Philosophy from Stanford, but that diploma had been lost many years ago. He had tried teaching but didn't like the constraints of a job. He liked to drink and travel. So, at 30, he became a traveling man and his family went years without hearing from him.

Now he lived with his sister Anne in a tiny single-wide trailer, perched on the side of a steep, sagebrush covered hill. The view was breathtaking and the road steep and difficult to drive up.

Jack's room must have originally been the den. It was basically a 10 X 10 room minus a door, and was located across from the laundry room. A bed, a TV, an overflowing bookshelf, an oxygen condenser and a chair filled the room to capacity.

All visitors had to walk through the laundry room to enter the trailer, making it perfect for Jack. He could see everyone as they came in or went out, and was always willing to share a story with them.

The hospice nursing staff resolved Jack's pain quickly. He was open to all their suggestions and enjoyed their regular visits. He loved chemistry and put the nurses through their paces talking about why a specific medication worked for a specific symptom, and why another one would not. Jack loved the regular hospice visits, and even in his weakened state he loved to flirt.

The hospice visits were wonderful for Anne, too. She became proficient in giving Jack the medication he so desperately needed. She knew she had the support of a nurse twenty-four hours a day, and that made her feel confident she could see her brother through his journey.

As a social worker one of my jobs is to identify what patients might want, in order to make their life better. I asked Jack what I could do for him. He said he was bored with TV and that he had no future and got tired of just waiting for the end. He wanted to know if I could carry on a good conversation and occasionally make him laugh. That was the start of my relationship with Jack. I told him my grasshopper joke.

"A grasshopper walks into a bar and climbs up onto a bar stool. The bartender says, 'Hey, did you know there's a drink named after you?' The grasshopper looked at him, surprised, and replied, 'Really, you have a drink named Fred?'" It was the only joke I knew, and he graciously laughed.

Each week I visited him and we talked about everything. He shared his views on politics, the ways of the world, jokes, the environment, ridiculous TV programs, and always stories about his incredible adventures. He loved to laugh, and through these visits I got to know him as a sweet man who had lived a life of adventure, and now was dying at 66.

Jack's symptoms were difficult to keep under control because they were always changing. When he became anxious he would become extremely short of breath and feel like he was suffocating. This could be controlled with medication but he didn't want to take the medication unless he absolutely had to.

So I helped him develop another way to deal with it, using visualizations. It's a wonderfully empowering tool and can often be very helpful controlling anxiety and stress.

We identified his favorite places. Using his glorious descriptions, I helped him create visualizations and added some deep breathing techniques to use whenever his cancer symptoms threatened to over take him.

We also created sweet, gentle visualizations where he was floating in a warm ocean, sea birds flying above, just for pleasure.

I recorded the visualizations on his tape recorder, so he could listen to them any time he wanted to drift away. Jack followed all my suggestions, and found that by visualizing he could control his anxiety and reduce his shortness of breath.

Jack was not a religious man but he was spiritual. He believed that our souls live on after death. After exploring his beliefs during many profound conversations, I discovered he didn't have a clear vision of what was going to happen after death. He told me he was afraid to think about the actual end. But if I wanted to talk about it, he was game.

A clear vision of what happens at the end of life isn't required but it's often helpful in reducing fear in the person who's in the process of dying. Once we started talking about dying and what would happen next, Jack surprised himself and actually had a lot to say. Jack identified what he thought were important ingredients for his cycle of life.

This became his explanation of where he was going after his life: "You need water, chemical building blocks like carbon, oxygen, hydrogen, nitrogen and an energy source."

He said he believed that there was a new world out there just waiting for him. He said, "It's just a moment away." And then he described where he was going and how his new world would look.

Jack specifically liked dragonflies, the big florescent blue ones. We could see them through his bedroom window, flying around. They often buzzed right up against the glass.

He said he wouldn't mind becoming one himself and laughed a deep, hearty laugh. Just then he said, "I've got it! The adult dragonfly drops her fertilized egg onto the surface of the water. The tiny egg floats down to the bottom of the lake, and from that tiny egg it develops into a nymph. He spends a lifetime in the pond, wiggling around, eating, drinking, chasing women, smoking, traveling the rails, sometimes with his buddies and sometimes all alone."

"Eventually after a lifetime he starts to feel old and cranky. His body doesn't fit anymore, it's dry and brittle and his feet keep swelling."

Jack chuckled, looking at his own feet. "In his discomfort he crawls out of the water trying to find a solution and some relief. He stays at the edge of the lake for a while, feeling out of place but not knowing what else to do. "

"Then his body starts to dry and crack, exposing parts of him that he has never seen before. He realizes that he is florescent blue underneath his ugly gray husk and starts to feel a tiny bit of hope. Once the cracking is complete, the old exterior husk falls away, leaving a healthy adult dragonfly. He can't believe it! The old aches and pains are gone and he's beautiful!"

"He stands tall, admiring his gossamer wings shining in the sunlight. Without a thought, he lifts his bright blue muscular body up from the shore and flies away, free to explore his new world."

Jack continued his story, "His empty husk blows back into the lake and slowly sinks down past his friends. They can't believe it! They didn't see it coming and they are at a loss."

"They say, 'Hey, that looks like Jack! Was he sick? I didn't even know something was wrong.' Eventually they realize that Jack is dead and he's not coming back. They have a wake at his favorite pond bar and tell funny stories about him. "Everyone raises their glass, for Jack, just one more time."

Jack smiled. "His friends go on with their wet pond life, not realizing that Jack has just gone through metamorphosis."

Jack went on, "In reality he has entered a new dimension; he now lives in a different world. He flies fast with his new wings and florescent blue body. He's eating bugs, finding new places to explore, and landing on plants to drink the nectar of life."

Jack stopped for a minute and said, eyes twinkling, "When I become a dragonfly I'm going to chase a lot more dragonfly women and see the world in style, on my beautiful see-through wings."

When he was done he was satisfied, and seemed to know exactly where he was headed. Jack was smiling his full smile. He loved the visualization. I had recorded the whole story so he could listen to it again whenever he wanted to.

The last time I saw him, we talked a lot about his death transition.

When Jack spoke he became short of breath and had to stop every few words. As he sat on the edge of his bed, his feet didn't look real. They were swollen and shiny and his toes could no longer be seen. It was obvious from his swollen legs that his heart was struggling, too. He had good pain control, which was a relief.

During one visit Jack told me he'd had four close calls in the past few weeks and knew he wasn't going to survive the fifth one.

He said the first close call scared him, but his sister gave him the emergency medication and he made it through. The second one he fought, didn't tell Anne, and visualized his happy place. The third one was scary, but he understood what was happening and the hospice nurse arrived in a hurry. He loved the fact that he could be treated in his home in his own bed. "The fourth," he said, "I just wasn't ready to go yet."

He let Anne know when it first started and the on-call nurse was able to forestall the inevitable one more time. He was sure the fifth one would take him. He said he was ready, and I knew he meant it.

We talked a little more and I told him how much I had enjoyed knowing him and his great mind and brilliant conversations. He smiled and said he felt better at that moment than he had during the past week.

I noticed his eyes smiling out from under his hat and thought to myself, what a gentle man I have had the honor of knowing. I wished him good evening and turned to leave.

As the laundry room door was closing, Jack, hat pulled down over his ears, hair sticking out, and his dark eyes sparkling, smiled and announced, "Joanne, I love you."

I said, "Jack, I love you, too." We both smiled as the door closed. Somehow I knew that would be the last time I would see him.

Jack died later that night. The hospice nurse and Anne were by his side.

I went to his home the next morning for a condolence call. Anne said Jack had had another event later that evening. She said she knew he was dying, even though the nurse was doing everything she could. She told me that towards the end, Jack had motioned for her to turn on the recorder.

He laid back, shut his eyes and whispered, "Dragonfly." It was his last breath.

Anne said she had been ready for that day to come. She laughed and added, "He always was one for theatrics."

So Jack had floated up to the water's edge, climbed onto the shore and left his old worn out body. He stood on the surface of our world and flew away, a big florescent dragonfly. He was finally free and out of pain, on to another adventure in another world. Jack left this world with dignity and understanding, and I hoped I had made him laugh a little.

One Year Later

I see Jack even today in my travels, at the edge of a pond or river stream, and even in my garden. When I see that big florescent flash I remember a wonderful man who was willing to look at his own death without blinking.

Anne is doing very well. She accessed the grief support hospice offered and has assimilated her brother's loss into her life. She is very proud that she was there for her brother and that she was part of helping him leave this world in style.

Anne said she listened to the dragonfly recording a few times and was glad to still be able to hear Jack's voice. She said she disagreed a little with his logic, though. And then she smiled. Her smile looked a lot like Jack's.

She said proudly, "I'm going to become a damselfly!"

Hospice is available to anyone whom the doctor believes has six months or less to live. Jack was able to live until his death exactly the way he wanted to, at home, with support from his sister.

When you are inspired by some great purpose or some extraordinary project, all your thoughts break their bonds; your mind transcends limitations, your consciousness expands in every direction, and you find yourself in a new, great and wonderful world. Dormant forces, faculties and talents become alive, and you discover yourself to be a greater person by far than you ever dreamed yourself to be.

Patanjali (c. 1st to 3rd century BC)

Resources

Advanced Directives
(also known as Durable Power of Attorney for Health Care)
A form where you appoint someone you love or trust to speak for you
if you can't. Everyone over 18 years old should have one of these forms
completed and in a safe place.

Free online http://www.doyourproxy.org

Advanced Directive Free for each state.
http://www.caringinfo.org/stateaddownload

AIDS
A non-profit organization for the free and open exchange of information
in the fight against *AIDS*.
http://www.aids.org

American Cancer Society Cancer
facts and figures plus health information. http://www.cancer.org

American Heart Association

Learn more about the American *Heart* Association's efforts to reduce death caused by cardiovascular disease.

http://www.americanheart.org

American Lung Association

A national, voluntary health organization that works to prevent lung disease and promote lung health.

http://www.lungusa.org

Alzheimer's Prevention

Alzheimer's Foundation of America.

Toll free 866-AFA.8484 http://www.alzprevention.org

Compassionate Friends

Death of a Child: a self-help support organization which aids bereaved families after the death of a child.

http://www.compassionatefriends.org/home.aspx

Care giving resources http://sharethecare.org/

Caregiver by State Resource

Intended to help you locate government, non-profit, and private programs in your area. http://www.caregiver.org/caregiver/jsp/fcn_content_node.jsp?nodeid=2083

Caregiving support access referrals for homecare, adult daycare, and or inhome services, senior housing, assisted living or nursing homes. http://eldercarelink.com

Funeral services
Check with your local funeral home. Many of them can make whatever you want a reality.
http://funeralresources.com

Body Donation:
The generous gift of your body after death is a compassionate alternative to a traditional funeral. The place where you donate will usually cover all costs associated with donation. If you search for "body donation" on the Internet you will find a list of companies. Always research these companies. Most are excellent but as usual, customer beware. If you live in a rural community make sure they will make all arrangements to pick up the remains, any time, day or night, without incurring charges.

Choosing a Final Resting Place
There is a growing trend for more creative options for end-of-life disposition. One can be cremated and then scattered or buried at sea, or kept in a commemorative urn, or even have part of one's remains sent into space or be made into works of art or jewelry. Find more suggestions at:
http://dying.about.com/od/finalrestingplace/p/resting_place.htm

Medicare
Toll free (800) 633-4227 www.medicare.gov

Medicaid services (Low income elder or disabled medical coverage)
(800)-633-4227
This is a voice-automated system. You will need to request information about Medicaid and, when prompted, say the state you live in. After doing so, it will announce the number of the Medicaid office closest to where you live. www.cms.hhs.gov/medicaideligibility

Medi-Cal (Medicaid for California) http://dhcs.ca.gov/services/medical or contact your local county welfare office.

Medicare Rights Center
They are responsible for helping to ensure access to affordable health care for older adults and people with disabilities through counseling, educational programs and public policy initiatives. http://www.medicarerights.org

Hospice or Palliative Care
National Hospice and Palliative Care Organization
http://www.nhpco.org/templates/1/homepage.cfm

Caring Connections, a program of the National Hospice and Palliative Care Organization (NHPCO), provides free, in-depth resources and information on hospice care, advance directives, including state-by-state forms and much more. To locate a hospice provider in your area, go to: http://www.caringinfo.org/CaringForSomeone/Hospice/ChoosingAHospice.htm

National Hospice Foundation
http://www.nationalhospicefoundation.org/home.cfm

National Hospice and Palliative Care Organization's Help Line
Toll free 800-568-8898
An International Association for Hospice & Palliative Care. promoting Hospice and Palliative Care Worldwide. http://www.hospicecare.com

World Health Organization

WHO is the directing and coordinating authority for health within the United Nations system. It is responsible for providing leadership on global health matters, shaping the health research agenda, setting norms and standards, articulating evidence-based policy options, providing technical support to countries, and monitoring and assessing health trends.

http://www.who.int/cancer/palliative/en/

Recommended Reading

The Four Things that Matter Most, by Ira Byock. Why wait until we or someone we love is dying to say the things that matter most?

Final Gifts: Understanding the Special Awareness, Needs, and Communication of the Dying by Maggie Callanan & Patricia Kelly. Stories about near death awareness. A sweet book that is empowering both to caregivers and the dying.

Handbook for Mortals, by Joanne Lynn, MD and Joan Harrold, M.D. A comprehensive and authoritive guide to end-of-life care written for a general audience by a team that includes some of the top specialists.

The Needs of the Dying: A Guide for Bringing Hope, Comfort, and Love to Life's Final Chapter. by David Kessler, M.D. A compassionate and practical look at the issues of the dying patient.

At Home With Dying by Merrill Collett . A practical guide addressing the physical, emotional, and spiritual skills needed to care for someone who is terminally ill. Based on the principles that guide the San Francisco Zen Center.

And A Time to Die, How American Hospitals Shape the End of Life, by Sharon R. Kaufman. Interesting reading by a medical anthropologist, revealing how American hospitals shape the end of life.

Final Choices: Seeking a Good Death by Michael Vitez. Intended for general audience, this book helps health care consumers examine choices in medical care, hospice alternatives, home care, assisted suicide, and related issues.

When Children Die: Improving Palliative and End-Of-Life Care for Children and Their Families, by Marilyn J. Field.

Peaceful Dying, by Daniel R. Tobin, M.D. A step-by-step guide to preserving dignity, choices, and inner peace at the end of life.

Medicine and Care of the Dying by Milton J. Lewis. An historical examination of how approaches to dying have changed in recent years, reflecting the growth in palliative medicine as a new medical speciality.

Palliative Care and Perspectives by James L. Hallenbeck M.D. A wonderful book that covers all the major points in palliative care, giving the reader practical and useful information.

Morrie: In His Own Words, by Morrie Schwartz, Advice about how the dying want to be treated from the subject of *Tuesdays with Morrie*.

For As Long As I Can: a Son's Memoir of his Father's Dying Request by Roland E. Cavanaugh. A rich, touching journey of a father's last challenge and his son's attempt to honor him.

Understanding Your Grief: Ten Essential Touchstones for Finding Hope and Healing Your Heart, by Alan Wolfelt, Ph.D.   Excellent book and complete program. This book offers a step-by-step guide though grief. Highly recommended. Joanne uses Wolfelt's books as a model for her grief support groups.

Guiding Your Child Through Grief by Mary Ann Emswiler, MA., M.P.S. and James P. Emswiler, M.A., M.ED. Offers expert advice on how to help a child grieve the death of a parent or sibling. Covers issues such as complicated grief, caring for caregivers, tips for teachers, step-parents and health professionals.

The Grieving Garden: Living with the Death of a Child by Suzanne Redfern. An inspiring book for parents who are grieving the loss of a child.

Sad Isn't Bad: A Good Grief Guidebook for Kids Dealing with Loss. by Michaelene Mundy, illustrated by R. W. Alley. Nice summary of the grief process, written for a young audience though the material is valuable for all ages.

Life after Loss: Conquering Grief and finding Hope by Raymond Moody Jr., M.D. & Dianne Arcangel. Leading experts explain near death experiences and after death experiences. The authors show how the grieving process can transform fear and grief into spiritual enlightenment.

Goodbye, Friend: Healing Wisdom for Anyone Who Has Ever Lost a Pet by Gary Kowalski. A very short book for people looking for comfort after losing an elderly pet.

Coping with Sorrow on the Loss of Your Pet by Moira Anderson. For anyone who is struggling with the loss of a pet.

The Polar Express by Chris Van Allsburg. A sweet book full of wonder and fantasy. Everyone should have at least one copy in their library.

The Story of Ferdinand by Munro Lead, drawings by Robert Lawson. A fun story about a bull who loved to smell flowers.

Graceful Passages: A companion For Compassionate Transition. Wisdom of the World Series

Books For Living Life to the Fullest

Once Upon a Vine, The Secret Stories of California's Artisan Wineries by Judy Reynolds. These are not just wine stories, but life stories to treasure. www.OnceUponaVineTheBook.com

Papa Mike's Cook Island Handbook by Mike Hollywood. A wonderfully humorus and informative book about traveling to the Cook Islands.

Papa Mike's Palau Island Handbook, by Mike Hollywood. Travel to the far corners of paradise. Do it now!

Holy Health by Percy McManus. This book catalogs 144 illnesses, connecting the emotional and spiritual reasons why a person becomes sick and how to address the solution on all three levels.

Shortcuts to Health by Percy McManus. A daily appointment calendar that displays a nutritional tip for every day of the year. www.healthexcellence. com

Soups Smoothies and Delectable Drinks by Angela Treat Lyon. www. EFTBooks.com

*Man's mind once stretched by a new idea, never regains its
original dimension.*

Oliver Wendell Holmes

What are Meridian Tapping Techniques?

If you're not familiar with Meridian Tapping Techniques, you must be wondering what it's all about.

Meridian Tapping, otherwise known as MTT, is a healing technique based on the ancient Chinese art of acupuncture. But instead of needles, your fingers tap on well-established points on your body. These spots are known as meridian points. Meridians are pathways of energy which flow through our bodies. There are twelve major pathways. Each one passes through a specific organ of the body, such as the heart, liver, lungs or kidneys. The entire system is interconnected, energy traveling from one meridian to the next, moving in a continuous flow. These meridians are linked to larger fields in our bodies, called chakras.

Chakras are energy centers that run from the base of the spine to the top, or crown, of your head. The word *chakra* is a Sanskrit word, meaning wheel or disc. There are seven major chakras, each a circular wheel of light spinning in your energy system, associated with certain body parts.

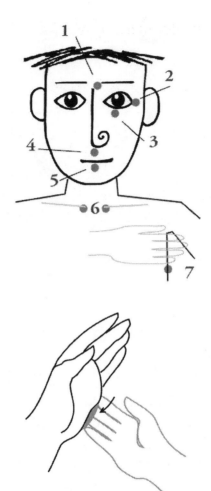

Example of meridian spots that are tapped to release blocked energy.

Illustrations by Angela Treat Lyon, http://AngelaTreatLyon.com

The Development of Meridian Tapping

It is believed the Chinese people discovered the human energy system thousands of years ago. This discovery eventually led to the development of acupuncture. As time went on different techniques were developed and improved upon. Energy meridian tapping, which involved gentle tapping or touching the meridian points, is thought to have started with George Goodheart, a chiropractor who discovered that touching acupuncture spots reduced pain. John Diamond (1985), a psychiatrist, and Roger Callahan (1987), a psychologist, both experimented with meridian tapping to treat mental illness. Fred Gallo (1998) and Gary Craig (1995) both developed their own style of meridian tapping. Gary Craig was very successful in getting the information out to the public and has helped train clinicians and many others all over the world. From Gary Craig and the information he provided, I learned about meridian tapping, and attended trainings, seminars and one-on-one coaching from a variety of Meridian Tapping Masters.

MTT incorporates an emotional element to the healing process, addressing unresolved emotional issues as the likely cause of physical disease and personal performance limitations. MTT can quickly realign the meridians that hold negative memories, and disconnect their attached physical discomforts.

It is a simple, yet elegant, technique. It can be taught in a few hours and be self directed, or it can be done with a trained practitioner. MTT often provides results to clients who believe there is nothing else they can do to reduce their suffering.

If you would like to get more education or arrange for a Meridain Tapping session, please go to: www.eftjoanne.com.

Joanne Harvey lives with her husband Jim, in Northern California. She holds a Bachelor degree in Psychology and a Masters degree in Medical Social Work. Joanne is a hospice social worker, life coach and meridian practitioner with years of experience guiding clients through the challenges of life and self-discovery.

12001254R00090

Made in the USA
Charleston, SC
04 April 2012